A GIFT FROM
GRACE TO YOU

ONE FOUNDATION

One Foundation: Essays on the Sufficiency of Scripture copyright © 2019 by Grace to You. All rights reserved. No portion of this book may be reproduced in any form without the written permission of the copyright owner, except for brief excerpts quoted in critical reviews. Each chapter remains the intellectual property of its author.

All Scripture quotations in this book, except those noted otherwise, are from the New American Standard Bible® (NASB), Copyright © 1960, 1962, 1963, 1968, 1971, 1972, 1973, 1975, 1977, 1995 by The Lockman Foundation, and are used by permission. www.Lockman.org Scripture quotations marked NKJV are taken from the New King James Version®. Copyright © 1982 by Thomas Nelson. Used by permission. All rights reserved. Scripture quotations marked ESV are taken from the ESV® Bible (The Holy Bible, English Standard Version®), copyright © 2001 by Crossway, a publishing ministry of Good News Publishers. Used by permission. All rights reserved. Scripture quotations marked KJV are taken from the King James Version of the Bible.

Edited by Jeremiah Johnson

Designed by Melinda Welch

Chapter from *What Is Reformed Theology?* by R. C. Sproul, copyright © 1997. Used by permission of Baker Books, a division of Baker Publishing Group.

Chapter from *The Inerrant Word* by John MacArthur, copyright © 2016. Used by permission of Crossway, a publishing ministry of Good News Publishers. www.crossway.org

Chapter from *Romans: An Exposition of Chapter 1* by Dr. Martyn Lloyd-Jones, copyright © 1985. Used by permission of the Banner of Truth Trust. www.banneroftruth.org

ISBN: 978-0-578-54235-5

Printed in the United States of America

Valencia, California

CONTENTS

FOREWORD

On February 9, 1969, John MacArthur preached his first sermon at Grace Community Church. That sermon, titled "How to Play Church," was recorded on reel-to-reel tape, effectively launching John's media ministry—what we know today as Grace to You.

The special volume you hold in your hands was compiled to celebrate fifty years of John MacArthur's verse-by-verse Bible teaching through the ministry of Grace to You. However, in keeping with John's distaste for personal accolades and acclaim, this book is not about him. In fact, we encouraged our contributors to leave his name out of their essays altogether. But as you will see, some could not help themselves.

Instead, we wanted this book to put the emphasis where John believes it always belongs—on the Word of God. Specifically, we wanted to celebrate the aspects of Scripture's character and quality that have been the focal points of John's teaching, and to reflect the high view of God's Word that has marked and defined the ministry of Grace to You.

More than that, we wanted to illustrate what John MacArthur often says about his own teaching—that he is simply one in a long line of men who have sought faithfully to uphold the authority, inerrancy, perspicuity, and sufficiency of Scripture. To that end, some of the chapters we have included are from men who are already in glory but whose lives and ministries had a direct and tangible influence on John.

You will also note that we included a chapter from John himself, adapted from his 2016 book *The Inerrant Word*. Including a contribution from the honoree is unusual for a volume like this, but we felt it was an essential statement on the theme we want to highlight: the sufficiency of Scripture. To be completely honest, we at Grace to You all love John's classic sermon on Psalm 19 too much not to include it. After all, it is the best discourse on the sufficiency of Scripture we have seen since the Puritan era.

Just a brief word about the Grace to You staff: No one comes to work here by accident. The men and women the Lord has placed at Grace to You—along with those who have served here in the past, and especially our invaluable corps of volunteers—are all here because they have benefited from John MacArthur's verse-by-verse Bible teaching. Some of us had the privilege of growing up under John's pulpit teaching, while others found John's ministry relatively late in life. All of us were attracted to the prospect of reaching out to people with the same teaching that had already touched and transformed our lives. Everyone at Grace to You understands the spiritual value of John's teaching, because we all directly benefit from it ourselves.

That personal investment touches every aspect of the work we do. From the radio production crew to the customer service representatives; from the designers and programmers who maintain our website to the shipping team who often arrive before dawn to fill orders—we all understand the value of this ministry, and we count it a great privilege to serve the Lord by serving you.

While the assembly of this volume was a team effort, a few names merit special mention. Thanks to Jessica Sum and Steve Ostini for their invaluable editorial work on this manuscript, and to Cameron Buettel for his input and assistance with this project from inception to completion.

Hebrews 13:7 commands God's people, "Remember those who led you, who spoke the word of God to you; and considering the result of their conduct, imitate their faith." Our sincere hope is to obey that command with this volume. We hope it stokes your passion for the Word of God and prompts you to give thanks for all those who have faithfully taught it to you.

On behalf of the Grace to You staff, past and present, with inexpressible gratitude for our pastor-teacher, John MacArthur, and the manifold ways the Lord has sharpened and blessed us through him.

—Jeremiah Johnson
General Editor

No.1

BASED ON GOD'S WORD ALONE

BY R. C. SPROUL

"Unless I am convinced by Sacred Scripture or by evident reason, I will not recant. My conscience is held captive by the Word of God and to act against conscience is neither right nor safe." These immortal words were uttered by Martin Luther at the Diet of Worms. He was on trial for his life before the authorities of both church and state, charged with serious heresy. When commanded to recant his doctrine of justification by faith, he insisted that his doctrine was based on the Bible. In earlier debates with leading Roman Catholic theologians, Luther had been maneuvered into admitting that he thought it possible for both the pope and church councils to err.

Historians have frequently explained the Protestant Reformation by describing its material cause and its formal cause. Its material cause was the dispute over the doctrine of justification by faith alone (*sola fide*); its formal cause, the dispute over biblical authority (*sola Scriptura*).

The principle of *sola Scriptura* lurked in the background throughout the debate over justification. Luther's refusal to recant at Worms brought it into the foreground. From that point on, *sola Scriptura* became a battle cry for Protestants.

The term *sola Scriptura* simply means "by Scripture alone." This slogan declared the idea that only the Bible has the authority to bind the consciences of believers. Protestants did recognize other forms of authority, such as church offices, civil magistrates, and church creeds and confessions. But they saw these authorities as being derived from and subordinate to the authority of God. None of these lesser authorities was deemed absolute because all of them were capable of error. God alone is infallible. Fallible authorities cannot bind the conscience absolutely; that right is reserved to God and His Word alone.

A common misunderstanding is that the Reformers believed in the infallible authority of Scripture while the Roman Catholic Church believed only in the infallible authority of the church and her tradition. This is a distortion of the controversy. At the time of the Reformation, both sides acknowledged the infallible authority of the Bible. The question was this: Is the Bible the *only* infallible source of special revelation?

Roman Catholics taught that there are two sources of infallible special revelation: Scripture and tradition. Since they attributed this authority to the tradition of the church, they did not permit any person to interpret the Bible in a way that was contrary to this tradition. That is precisely what Luther did, leading to his excommunication and the condemnation of his doctrine.

The Reformers agreed there are two kinds of divine revelation: *general* and *special*. General revelation, sometimes called *natural revelation*, refers to God's revelation of Himself in nature. The apostle Paul declares this in Romans:

> For the wrath of God is revealed from heaven against all ungodliness and unrighteousness of men, who suppress the truth in unrighteousness, because what may be known of God

> is manifest in them, for God has shown it to them. For since the creation of the world His invisible attributes are clearly seen, being understood by the things that are made, even His eternal power and Godhead, so that they are without excuse. (Rom. 1:18–20)[1]

As we have seen, this revelation is called "general" because of both its audience and its content. All people receive God's revelation in nature; not all have read Scripture (special revelation) or been exposed to its teaching. General revelation does not reveal the history of redemption or the person and work of Christ; special revelation does.

Though the Reformers distinguished between general and special revelation, they insisted there is only one written source of special revelation, the Bible. This is the *sola* of *sola Scriptura*. The chief reason for the word *alone* is the conviction that the Bible is inspired by God, while church creeds and pronouncements are the works of men. These lesser works may be accurate and brilliantly conceived, capturing the best insights of learned scholars, but they are not the inspired Word of God.

THE INSPIRATION OF SCRIPTURE

The Reformers held to a high view of the Bible's inspiration. The Bible is the Word of God, the *verbum Dei*, or the voice of God, the *vox Dei*. For example, John Calvin writes:

> When that which professes to be the Word of God is acknowledged to be so, no person, unless devoid of common sense and the feelings of a man, will have the desperate hardihood to refuse credit to the speaker. But since no daily responses are given from heaven, and the Scriptures are the

[1] Unless otherwise noted, Scripture quotations in this chapter are from the New King James Version.

> only records in which God has been pleased to consign his truth to perpetual remembrance, the full authority which they ought to possess with the faithful is not recognized, unless they are believed to have come from heaven, as directly as if God had been heard giving utterance to them.[2]

"As if" does not mean Calvin believed that the Bible had dropped down from heaven directly or that God Himself wrote the words on the pages of Scripture. Rather "as if" refers to the weight of divine authority that attends the Scriptures. This authority is rooted and grounded in the fact that Scripture was originally given under divine inspiration. This claim agrees with the Bible's own claim to authority: "All Scripture is given by inspiration of God, and is profitable for doctrine, for reproof, for correction, for instruction in righteousness, that the man of God may be complete, thoroughly equipped for every good work" (2 Tim. 3:16–17).

Paul's declaration of Scripture's inspiration refers to its origin. He uses the Greek word *theopneustos*, which means "God-breathed." Though the word is usually translated "inspired," which means "breathe in," technically *theopneustos* refers to a breathing out, which might more accurately be translated "expired." Paul is saying that Scripture is "expired" or "breathed out" by God. This is not a mere quibble. It is obvious that for inspiration to take place there must first be expiration. A breathing out must precede a breathing in. The point is that the work of divine inspiration is accomplished by a divine expiration. Since Paul says that Scripture is breathed out by God, Scripture's origin or source must be God Himself.

When Calvin and others speak of Scripture's inspiration, they refer to the way in which God enabled the human authors of Scripture to function so that they wrote every word under divine superintendence. The doctrine of inspiration declares that God

[2] John Calvin, *Institutes of the Christian Religion*, 2 vols., trans. Henry Beveridge (1845; reprint, Grand Rapids, MI: Eerdmans, 1964), 1:68 (1.7.1).

enabled the human writers of Scripture to be agents of divine revelation so that what they wrote was not only their writing but in a higher sense the very Word of God. The origin of Scripture's content is found ultimately in God.

Much debate has raged concerning the exact mode or method of this divine inspiration. Some have contended for a mechanical inspiration or dictation, reducing the human authors to robotic machines or passive stenographers who merely recorded the words dictated to them by God.

But the Scriptures themselves make no such claim. The mode or precise manner of divine inspiration is not spelled out. The crucial point of the biblical claim to authority is that God is the source who breathes out His Word. It is clear from a study of the Bible itself that the authors' individual styles remain intact. The inspiration of the Bible refers then to the divine superintendence of Scripture, preserving it from the intrusion of human error. It refers to God's preserving His Word through the words of human authors.

THE INFALLIBILITY OF SCRIPTURE

The Reformers were convinced that, because the Bible has its origin in God and was superintended by His inspiration, it is infallible. Infallibility refers to its indefectibility or the impossibility of its being in error. That which is infallible is incapable of failing. We attribute infallibility to God and His work because of His nature and character. With respect to God's nature, He is deemed to be omniscient. With respect to His character, He is deemed to be holy and altogether righteous.

Theoretically we can conceive of a being who is righteous but limited in his knowledge. Such a being could make mistakes in his utterances, not because of a desire to deceive or defraud but due to his lack of knowledge. His would be honest mistakes. At the human level we understand that persons may make false statements without telling a lie. The difference between a lie and a simple mistake is at the level of intent. On the other hand, we can conceive of a being who is omniscient but evil. This being could not make a mistake due to lack of knowledge, but could tell a lie. This would clearly involve evil or malicious intent. Since God is both omniscient and morally perfect, however, He is incapable of telling a lie or making an error.

When we say the Bible is infallible in its origin, we are merely ascribing its origin to a God who is infallible. This is not to say that the biblical writers were intrinsically or in themselves infallible. They were human beings who, like other humans, proved the axiom *Errare humanum est*, "To err is human." It is precisely because humans are given to error that, for the Bible to be the Word of God, its human authors required assistance in their task.

At issue in our day is the question of Scripture's inspiration. On this point some theologians have tried to have their cake and eat it too. They affirm the Bible's inspiration while at the same time denying its infallibility. They argue that the Bible, in spite of its divine inspiration, still errs. The idea of divinely inspired error is one to choke on. We shrink in horror at the notion that God inspires error. To inspire error would require either that God is not omniscient or that He is evil.

Perhaps what is in view in the idea of inspired error is that the inspiration, though proceeding from a good and omniscient God, is simply ineffectual to the task at hand. That is, it fails to accomplish its intended purpose. In this case another attribute of God, His omnipotence, is negotiated away. Perhaps God is simply unable to superintend the writing of Scripture with sufficient power to overcome the human authors' propensity for error.

Surely it would make more sense to deny inspiration altogether than to conjoin inspiration with error. To be sure, most critics of the Bible's infallibility take their axes to the root of the tree and reject inspiration altogether. This seems a more honest and logical approach. It avoids the impiety of denying foundational attributes to God Himself.

Let us examine briefly a formula that has had some currency in our day: "The Bible is the Word of God, which errs." Now let us expunge some of these words. Remove "The Bible is" so that the formula reads: "The Word of God, which errs." Now erase "The Word of" and "which." The result is "God errs." To say the Bible is the Word of God that errs is clearly to indulge in impious doublespeak. If it is the Word of God, it does not err. If it errs, it is not the Word of God. Surely we can have a word *about* God that errs, but we cannot have a word *from* God that errs.

That the Scripture has its origin in God is claimed repeatedly by Scripture. One example is found in Paul's epistle to the Romans. Paul identifies himself as "a servant of Jesus Christ, called to be an apostle, separated to the gospel of God" (Rom. 1:1). In the phrase "the gospel of God," the word *of* is a genitive indicating possession. Paul is speaking not merely of a gospel that is *about* God, but of a gospel belonging *to* God. It is God's possession and it comes from Him. In a word, Paul is declaring that the gospel he preaches is not from men or of human invention; it is given by divine revelation. The whole controversy over the inspiration and infallibility of the Bible is fundamentally a controversy about supernatural revelation. Reformed theology is committed to Christianity as a revealed faith, a faith that rests not on human insight but on information that comes to us from God Himself.

THE INERRANCY OF SCRIPTURE

In addition to affirming the Bible's infallibility, Reformed theology describes the Bible as inerrant. Infallibility means that something *cannot* err, while inerrancy means that it *does not* err. Infallibility describes ability or potential. It describes something that cannot happen. Inerrancy describes actuality.

For example, I could score 100 percent on a spelling test. In this limited experience I was "inerrant"; I made no mistakes on the test. This would not warrant the conclusion that I am therefore infallible. Errant human beings do not always err. They sometimes, indeed often do, err because they are not infallible. An infallible person would never err simply because infallibility as such precludes the very possibility of error.

In our day some scholars have asserted that the Bible is infallible but not inerrant. This creates no small amount of confusion. As we have seen, *infallible* is the stronger of the two words.

Why then have these scholars preferred the word *infallible?* The answer is probably located somewhere in the emotive realm. The term *inerrancy* is frowned on in certain academic circles. It is loaded with pejorative baggage. The term is often associated with unsophisticated and unscholarly types of fundamentalism. On the other hand, the term *infallibility* has a history of academic respectability, particularly in Roman Catholic scholarship. People may reject the Roman Catholic view of infallibility, but they do not identify it with backwoods, primitive theology. Jesuits, for example, do not suffer from a reputation of unsophisticated scholarship. To escape guilt by association with anti-intellectual circles, some have retreated from the term *inerrancy* and taken refuge in the term *infallibility*. If in the process *infallibility* is redefined to mean something less than *inerrancy*, however, then the shift in nomenclature is a dishonest subterfuge.

Though both *inerrancy* and *infallibility* have been integral to historic Reformed theology, the modern controversy over the Bible's trustworthiness has led others to argue that the concept of inerrancy was not advocated by the magisterial Reformers, but instead was originated by scholastic or rationalistic theologians of the seventeenth century. Though it may be accurate to say that the term *inerrancy* came into vogue later, it is by no means accurate to assert that the concept is absent from the works of sixteenth-century Reformers. Let us note a few observations from Martin Luther:

> The Holy Spirit Himself and God, the Creator of all things, is the Author of this book.[3]

[3] Martin Luther, *What Luther Says: An Anthology*, ed. Ewald M. Plass, 3 vols. (St Louis, MO: Concordia, 1959), 1:62.

Scripture, although also written of men, is not of men nor from men, but from God.[4]

He who would not read these stories in vain must firmly hold that Holy Scripture is not human but divine wisdom.[5]

The Word must stand, for God cannot lie; and heaven and earth must go to ruins before the most insignificant letter or tittle of His Word remains unfulfilled.[6]

We intend to glory in nothing but Holy Scripture, and we are certain that the Holy Spirit cannot oppose or contradict Himself.[7]

St. Augustine says in the letter to St. Jerome . . . I have learned to hold only the Holy Scripture inerrant.[8]

In the books of St. Augustine one finds many passages which flesh and blood have spoken. And concerning myself I must also confess that when I talk apart from the ministry, at home, at table, or elsewhere, I speak many words that are not God's Word. That is why St. Augustine, in a letter to St. Jerome, has put down a fine axiom—that only Holy Scripture is to be considered inerrant.[9]

---

[4] Ibid., 1:63.

[5] Ibid., 1:67.

[6] Ibid., 1:68.

[7] Ibid., 1:72.

[8] Ibid., 1:87.

[9] Ibid., 1:88.

It is clear that the concept of inerrancy was not a late invention. It is attested to in antiquity, not only in men such as St. Augustine, but in Irenaeus as well. Luther cites Augustine's view with manifest approval. The same approbation is found profusely in John Calvin's writings.

Clearly inerrancy and infallibility do not extend to copies or translations of Scripture. Reformed theology restricts inerrancy to the original manuscripts of the Bible, or the *autographa*. The *autographa*, the initial works of the writers of Scripture, are not directly available to us today.

For this reason many scoff at the doctrine of inerrancy, saying it is a moot point since it cannot be verified or falsified without access to the original manuscripts. This criticism misses the point altogether. We carry no brief for the inspiration of copyists or translators. The original revelation is the chief concern of the doctrine of inerrancy. Though we do not possess the autographs themselves, we can reconstruct them with remarkable accuracy. The science of textual criticism demonstrates that the existing text is remarkably pure and exceedingly reliable.

Suppose the normative yardstick housed at the National Bureau of Standards were to perish in a fire. Would we no longer be able to determine the distance of three feet with accuracy? With the multitude of existing copies, we could reconstruct with almost perfect accuracy the original yardstick. To restrict inerrancy to the original documents is to call attention to the source of biblical revelation: the agents who were inspired by God to receive His revelation and record it.

Reformed theology carries no brief for the infallibility of translations. We who read, interpret, or translate the Bible are fallible. The Roman Catholic Church adds another element of infallibility by claiming it for the church's interpretation of Scripture, especially when the pope speaks *ex cathedra* ("from the chair" of St. Peter). Through this adds a second tier of infallibility, the individual Roman Catholic is still left to interpret the infallible interpretation of the infallible Bible fallibly. Whereas Protestants are faced with a fallible interpretation of the church's fallible interpretation of the infallible Bible, Catholics assume a double level of infallibility.

What does the Bible's infallibility mean for the average Christian seeking to be guided by Scripture? If the final stage of receiving Scripture rests in our fallible understanding, why is the infallibility of the original documents so important? This is a practical question that bears heavily on the Christian life.

Suppose two people read a portion of Scripture and cannot agree on its meaning. Obviously one or both of them misunderstand the text. The debate between them is a debate between fallible people.

Suppose, however, that the text is clear and that neither person disputes its meaning. If one of them is convinced that the text is God's infallible revelation, then the question of whether he should submit to it is answered. If the other person is persuaded that the text itself (in its original transmission) is fallible, then he is under no moral obligation to be bound by it.

THE AUTHORITY OF SCRIPTURE

The issue of Scripture's inspiration and infallibility boils down to the issue of its authority. A famous bumper sticker reads as follows: "God says it. I believe it. That settles it."

What is wrong with this statement? It adds an element that is unsound. It suggests that the matter of biblical authority is not settled until the person believes the Bible. The slogan should read: "God says it. That settles it." If God reveals something, that revelation carries the weight of His authority. There is no higher authority. Once God opens His holy mouth, the matter is settled. This is axiomatic for Reformed theology.

The question of *sola Scriptura* is fundamentally one of authority. Here the supreme authority rests with the Bible, not the church; with God, not with man. This came home to me in a discussion with a former college roommate. We had lost contact with each other and had not seen each other for twenty years when we met again at a theology conference, where I was speaking on the topic of biblical authority. After the meeting we had dinner together and my friend said to me, "R. C., I don't believe in the infallibility of Scripture any more."

I asked him what he did still believe in from our earlier days. He said, "I still believe in Jesus as my Savior and Lord."

I indicated I was pleased to hear this, but proceeded to ask, "How does Jesus exercise His Lordship over your life?"

My friend, a bit perplexed by my question, asked, "What do you mean?"

"If Jesus is your Lord, then that means He exercises authority over you. How do you know how He wants you to live if not from the Bible?"

"From the teaching of the church," he replied.

Here was a "Protestant" who forgot what he was protesting. He had come full circle, jettisoning *sola Scriptura* and replacing it with the authority of the church. He placed the church above Scripture. This is not unlike what occurred in Rome. Though Rome did not deny Scripture's infallible authority as my friend did, she nevertheless in a real and critical sense subordinated Scripture to the church.

The subordination of Scripture was a burning issue among the Reformers. John Calvin said: "A most pernicious error has very generally prevailed—viz. that Scripture is of importance only in so far as conceded to it by the suffrage of the Church; as if the eternal and inviolable truth of God could depend on the will of men. With great insult to the Holy Spirit, it is asked, Who can assure us that the Scriptures proceeded from God[?] . . ."[10]

Calvin then reminds the reader that the Scriptures themselves (Eph. 2:20) declare that the church is established on the foundation of the apostles and prophets. He continues:

> Nothing, therefore, can be more absurd than the fiction, that the power of judging Scripture is in the Church, and that on her nod its certainty depends. When the Church receives it,

[10] Calvin, *Institutes of the Christian Religion*, 1:68–69 (1.7.1).

> and gives it the stamp of her authority, she does not make that authentic which was otherwise doubtful or controverted, but, acknowledging it as the truth of God, she, as in duty bound, shows her reverence by an unhesitating assent.[11]

Calvin has in view here the debate over the canon of Scripture. The sixty-six books of the Bible together comprise the canon of Scripture. The term *canon* means "measuring rod" or "rule." The Reformers did not recognize the books of the Apocrypha (written during the intertestamental period) as part of the canon. Rome did include the Apocrypha in the canon. Questions of which books are to be included in the canon were debated in the early church. In the final analysis the church recognized the books that now comprise the New Testament.

Since the church was involved in this process, some have argued that the Bible owes its authority to the church's authority and is therefore subordinate to the church's authority. This is the point Calvin so vigorously disputes. He declares that the church "does not make that authentic which was otherwise doubtful or controverted" but acknowledges it as God's truth. Calvin argues that there is a big difference between the church's recognizing the Bible's authority and the church's creating the Bible's authority. The church used the Latin term *recepimus*, which means "we receive," to acknowledge that books of the Bible are what they already were in themselves, the Word of God.

Luther wrote in a similar vein to Calvin concerning the relationship between the authority of the Bible and the authority of the church: "It is not the Word of God because the church says so; but that the Word of God might be spoken, therefore the church comes into being. The church does not make the Word, but it is made by the Word."[12] Luther goes on to say: "The church cannot give a book

---

[11] Ibid., 1:69.

[12] Luther, *What Luther Says*, 1:87.

more authority or dependability than it has of itself, just as it also approves and accepts the works of the fathers, but thereby does not establish them as good or make them better."[13]

Roman Catholics view the canon as an infallible collection of infallible books. Protestants view it as a fallible collection of infallible books. Rome believes the church was infallible when it determined which books belong in the New Testament. Protestants believe the church acted rightly and accurately in this process, but not infallibly.

This does not mean that Reformed theology doubts the canonical status of books included in the New Testament canon. Some Protestant theologians believe a special work of divine providence kept the church from error in this matter without imparting to the church any permanent or inherent infallibility.

The Reformed doctrine of *sola Scriptura*, then, affirms that the Bible is the sole written authority for the faith and life of God's people. We respect and submit to lesser ecclesiastical authority, but we are not bound by it absolutely as we are by biblical authority. This is the basis for the Reformation principle of *semper reformanda*, which indicates that the reformation of the church is an ongoing process. We are always called to seek more and more to bring our faith and practice into conformity to the Word of God.

THE INTERPRETATION OF SCRIPTURE

One great legacy of the Reformation is the principle of *private interpretation.* The Reformation effectively put the Bible into the hands of the laity. This was done at a great price, as some who translated the Bible into the vernacular paid for it with their lives. The right of private interpretation means that every Christian has the right to read and interpret the Bible for himself or herself. This does not give an individual the right to misinterpret or distort the Bible. The Bible is not a waxed nose to be twisted and shaped to

[13] Ibid.

fit one's fancy. With the right of private interpretation comes the responsibility of handling the Bible carefully and accurately. Nor does this right suggest that teachers, commentaries, and so forth are unnecessary or unhelpful. God has not gifted teachers for His church in vain.

The Bible is not to be interpreted arbitrarily. Fundamental rules of interpretation must be followed to avoid subjectivistic or fanciful interpretation, rules developed by the science of hermeneutics. The term *hermeneutics* is etymologically related to Hermes, a Greek god. Hermes was the messenger of the gods, corresponding to the Roman god Mercury. In mythology Mercury is often depicted with wings on his shoes to facilitate the delivery of messages with speed.

Hermeneutics prescribes the process by which we seek to understand a message. The Reformation established crucial rules of hermeneutics for interpreting the Bible. Perhaps the most crucial or central rule is the *analogy of faith*. This is the rule that Scripture is to interpret itself (*sacra Scriptura sui interpres*). We are to interpret Scripture by Scripture. If the Bible is the Word of God, then it is coherent and consistent with itself. God is not the author of confusion. He does not contradict Himself. We are not, therefore, to set one part of Scripture against another. What is unclear or obscure in one place may be clarified in another. We are to interpret the obscure in light of the clear, the implicit in light of the explicit, and the narrative in light of the didactic.

At a technical level the science of hermeneutics becomes quite complex. The biblical scholar must learn to recognize different forms of literature within the Scripture (genre analysis). For example, some parts of the Bible are in the form of historical narrative, while others are in the form of poetry. The interpretation of poetry differs from the interpretation of narrative. The Bible uses metaphor, simile, proverb, parable, hyperbole, parallelism, and many other literary devices that must be recognized in any serious work of interpretation.

One of the Reformation's chief accomplishments is the principle of the literal interpretation of Scripture. This concept has suffered from serious misunderstanding, having often been equated with a naive or wooden literalism. The actual principle, called *sensus literalis*, is that the Bible must be interpreted according to the manner in which it is written. *Literal* refers to the literary form of Scripture. Luther comments on this:

> Neither a conclusion nor a figure of speech should be admitted in any place of Scripture unless evident contextual circumstances or the absurdity of anything obviously militating against an article of faith require it. On the contrary, we must everywhere adhere to the simple, pure, and natural meaning of the words. This accords with the rules of grammar and the usage of speech (*usus loquendi*) which God has given to men. For if everyone is allowed to invent conclusions and figures of speech according to his own whim . . . nothing could to a certainty be determined or proved concerning any one article of faith that men could not find fault with by means of some figure of speech. Rather we must avoid as the most deadly poison all figurative language which Scripture itself does not force us to find in a passage.[14]

The principle of literal interpretation was intended to put an end to a method that had become popular in the Middle Ages, the *quadriga*. This was a method of interpretation by which four distinct meanings were sought for each biblical text: the literal, moral, allegorical, and analogical. This led to excessive allegorization and obfuscation of the text. By contrast, *sensus literalis* was designed to seek the plain sense of Scripture and to focus on one meaning. Though a text may have a multitude of applications, it has only one correct meaning.

The principle of *sensus literalis* is closely related to the *grammatico-historical* method of interpretation. This method focuses on the historical setting in which Scripture was written and pays close attention to the grammatical structure of the biblical text. In a broad sense this method means simply that the Bible is to be interpreted like

[14] Ibid., 1:93.

any other book. Its revelatory nature does not make it unlike any other book in that regard. It must still be read like any other book. In the Bible verbs are verbs and nouns are nouns. The normal structure of literature applies. Again Luther comments:

> The Holy Spirit is the plainest Writer and Speaker in heaven and on earth. Therefore His words can have no more than one, and that the most obvious, sense. This we call the literal or natural sense. But that the things meant by the plain sense of His plain Word may also mean something further and different, and thus one thing signifies another, is more than a question of words and languages. For this is true of all things outside Scripture, since all God's works and creatures are living signs and words of God, as St. Augustine and all the teachers declare. But we should not on this account say that Scripture or God's Word has more than one meaning.[15]

[15] Ibid., 1:91–92.

No.2

WHY YOU CAN BELIEVE THE BIBLE

BY VODDIE BAUCHAM

What is the most important question for a Christian to answer? You can probably think of some likely candidates. *What is the meaning of life? Where did we come from? What happens when you die?* Certainly many believers hope that someone will approach us with the bluntness of the rich young ruler and ask, "What shall I do to inherit eternal life?" (Luke 18:18). Those are all critical questions, and God's people need to be prepared to give thorough, biblical answers. As Peter says, we must "always [be] ready to make a defense to everyone who asks you to give an account for the hope that is in you, yet with gentleness and reverence" (1 Pet. 3:15).

But our answers to those questions inevitably point to a larger and more fundamental issue, one that has to do with the authority upon which we base our answers. Ultimately, the question all Christians have to answer is, "Why do you choose to believe the Bible?" Because everybody has their own set of beliefs and holy books, God's people need to be able to explain why they submit to the authority of Scripture. Why do we believe it truly is the Word of God?

BAD ANSWERS TO A GOOD QUESTION

Everywhere I travel around the globe, Christians young and old want to know how to respond to the fundamental question of biblical authority. Because the sad reality is, believers don't always give good answers to this vital question. In fact, there are some very bad answers that are frighteningly and frustratingly common.

We'll start with the worst: Call it the appeal to upbringing. This feeble answer usually comes from young believers, often when they're called upon to defend their faith for the first time. It is particularly common in college settings, when young Christians are confronted with questions about why they believe the Bible over the Koran, the Book of Mormon, or the writings of Confucius. Facing pushback from peers and professors, many students foolishly say, "I believe the Bible because that's how I was raised." Those careless words make the skeptic smile, as objections flood his mind. *Don't you know your parents are not always right? Couldn't the Bible be likewise fallible? Besides, plenty of people are raised to believe in a variety of books and faiths—why is yours any more credible than theirs?* And if your faith is simply the product of how you were raised, there is no way to answer those objections. Our best defense for the authority of Scripture cannot be, "My mom and dad told me . . ."

Sadly, that's not the only weak answer that routinely tumbles from the lips of believers attempting to defend the authority and veracity of the Bible. In such situations, too many Christians are prone to make the appeal to experience, saying something like, "I tried it, and it changed my life." Unlike the appeal to upbringing, many people today find this response compelling and winsome, because they believe experience trumps everything else. Who doesn't love a good tale of personal transformation?

But personal transformations don't always point back to the

truth. I know of a man who was born into a large family in the Midwest. His mother had mental problems, and his father was murdered while he was still young. He went to live with his sister in Boston, where he fell in with a crowd that was quite unsavory. Before long, he found himself in prison in Massachusetts. There he met some men who told him he needed to have his life changed. They told him about a messiah and urged him to believe and submit, but he couldn't. Then one night, he had a personal, vivid encounter with this messiah, and he finally bowed the knee. From that moment, his entire life changed. He became a model prisoner and received an early release. He went on to become one of the most famous preachers in America, and he was personally responsible for opening more than one hundred houses of worship. To this day, there are streets named after him in major cities across the country.

His name was Malcolm X, and he eventually came to realize that his messiah, the honorable Elijah Muhammad, was a fraud. So he abandoned the Nation of Islam to become an orthodox Muslim, and the Nation of Islam had him assassinated. That encounter in his prison cell was fraudulent, and yet he based everything on it. He had an experience, and it changed his life. But at the end of that life, he knew he was wrong.

The lie that changed his life was still a lie. Subjective stories of dramatic transformations are not a reliable test of the truth. By that logic, every sober alcoholic or addict rightly attributes just as much authority to the "higher powers" preached by AA or similar programs—they, too, tried it and it changed their lives.

God's people need to offer a stronger defense of His Word. We need to do better than citing our parental influences, or the subjective changes we've seen in our lives. We need to be able to give an account for why we are convinced that Scripture is, as it claims to be, the only authoritative Word of God.

Years ago I was speaking to group of Christian students at Dartmouth about apologetics and defending the faith, and the issue of how to answer this vital question of biblical authority came up. About a week later I received an email from a young lady who had attended that meeting. She wrote,

> It happened! It happened just like you said it would. I was in a biology class, and the discussion turned to evolution. The next thing I knew, my hand was in the air and I was voicing my objection. When the professor asked me why I disagreed, I told him I believe the Bible. I could almost see him salivating. His eyes got big, and he asked me, "Why do you believe the Bible?" And I gave him the answer that you gave us. I told him, "I choose to believe the Bible because it's a reliable collection of historical documents written by eyewitnesses during the lifetime of other eyewitnesses. They report supernatural events that took place in the fulfillment of specific prophecies and claimed that their writings are divine, rather than human, in origin." And the professor said, "I'll have to get back to you."

I want to teach you that same answer, so that you will be prepared the next time someone asks you why you believe the Bible. More than that, I want to show you where it comes from in Scripture.

Now you might ask why I would begin by appealing to the Bible. To put it simply, there is no higher authority than the Bible. If I were to appeal to another authority, I would be conceding the fact that there's a higher, more reliable authority than God's Word. However, I'm making the argument that Scripture is the highest authority. Therefore by definition, I cannot appeal to any other authority.

Some will immediately scoff at that notion, thinking that you can't successfully use the Bible to prove the Bible. They will write it off as circular reasoning. But understand that my goal is not to *prove* the Bible; my goal is to answer the question of why I choose to believe it. And the answer to that question lies in the Bible itself.

Specifically, we need to look to Peter's second epistle, where he explains why we can and should believe the Bible.

> For we did not follow cleverly devised tales when we made known to you the power and coming of our Lord Jesus Christ, but we were eyewitnesses of His majesty. For when He received honor and glory from God the Father, such an utterance as this was made to Him by the Majestic Glory, "This is My beloved Son with whom I am well-pleased"—and we ourselves heard this utterance made from heaven when we were with Him on the holy mountain. So we have the prophetic word made more sure, to which you do well to pay attention as to a lamp shining in a dark place, until the day dawns and the morning star arises in your hearts. But know this first of all, that no prophecy of Scripture is a matter of one's own interpretation, for no prophecy was ever made by an act of human will, but men moved by the Holy Spirit spoke from God. (2 Pet. 1:16–21)

That is Peter's response to questions about the authority and trustworthiness of Scripture. And it is from his answer that I have devised my own, that *I choose to believe the Bible because it's a reliable collection of historical documents written by eyewitnesses during the lifetime of other eyewitnesses. They report supernatural events that took place in fulfillment of specific prophecies and claimed that their writings are divine, rather than human, in origin.* That's how I respond when someone asks me why I believe the Bible.

I'll give it to you step by step, because every point here is important.

RELIABLE HISTORY

First, *the Bible is a reliable collection of historical documents.* This is critically important. It's important that it's reliable, it's important that it's a collection, and it's important that it's historical. Peter writes, "For we did not follow cleverly devised tales when we made known to you the power and coming of our Lord Jesus Christ" (2 Pet. 1:16). In other words, these weren't tall tales and myths. They weren't legends and rumors merely passed off as fact. What Scripture records about the Lord Jesus Christ is the truth about what He said and did. The account in the Bible is the true story.

And equally important is that that story is the product of several authors. The Bible is unlike many other holy books in that it is actually a collection. We don't have just one person who says he heard from God, and that everyone else needs to listen to him. The Bible isn't the work of just one individual making a claim, and that is critical when it comes to its credibility. It cannot be dismissed as the ravings of a lunatic, or the product of an overactive imagination.

Instead, God's Word is a collection of historical documents, written by more than forty authors coming from various walks of life. We have authors who were kings and generals, and others who were fishermen, tax collectors, and doctors. Those authors combined to write sixty-six volumes, covering the historical facts regarding countless people and events. Moreover, this collection was written on three continents (Asia, Africa, and Europe), in three languages (primarily Hebrew and Greek, with portions in Aramaic). And all of it was written over a period of more than fifteen hundred years.

Most Christians don't often think about the Bible in its component parts. We don't reflect on how it came together over the centuries—we just think of it as a single volume. But the fact that it is a collection of historical documents actually bolsters its credibility. Take the gospel of Luke for example. Luke describes how he assembled his account in the opening verses of his gospel.

> Inasmuch as many have undertaken to compile an account of the things accomplished among us, just as they were handed down to us by those who from the beginning were eyewitnesses and servants of the word, it seemed fitting for me as well, having investigated everything carefully from the beginning, to write it out for you in consecutive order, most excellent Theophilus; so that you may know the exact truth about the things you have been taught. (Luke 1:1–4)

Luke was not an eyewitness, nor did he claim to be. He wasn't a disciple. He was a historian—and a physician by trade—who recorded the testimonies he gathered from eyewitnesses. He investigated the events thoroughly, and wanted to provide an orderly, comprehensive account of them. That's why we get insight and perspective from Luke that the other gospels don't offer us. His goal was to record an accurate and chronological history of Christ's life and ministry.

The authors of the other gospel accounts had different priorities in mind. John's goal was evangelism. He made that clear in John 20:31, "These have been written so that you may believe that Jesus is the Christ, the Son of God; and that believing you may have life in His name." To that end, John organized his gospel around seven major signs that pointed to Christ's deity. Meanwhile, the gospel of Mark is focused on brevity. Mark's favorite words are "immediately" and "straightaway," as the apostle moves rapidly through the events of Christ's life. He followed the "just the facts" approach to communicating the story of Jesus with as little commentary as possible. Matthew, on the other hand, wrote to a primarily Jewish audience, and wanted to demonstrate that Jesus is the promised Jewish Messiah. That's why, for example, he began with the genealogy of Christ, pointing backward to emphasize His messianic credentials.

Some people like to scoff at the differences and supposed discrepancies between the four gospels, imagining that the variations somehow call into question their credibility. But the fact is that these four authors, writing at different times and from different perspectives, record many of the same details with astounding consistency. And together, the four Spirit-inspired gospel accounts give us a dynamic perspective on the events they describe. Like the rest of Scripture, they combine to give us a reliable collection of historical documents regarding the person and work of Christ.

FIRSTHAND REPORTS

Moreover, this reliable collection of historical documents was *written by eyewitnesses*. Peter makes that abundantly clear, "For we did not follow cleverly devised tales when we made known to you the power and coming of our Lord Jesus Christ, *but we were eyewitnesses of His majesty*" (2 Pet. 1:16, emphasis added). John makes a similar claim in his first epistle.

> What was from the beginning, what we have heard, what we have seen with our eyes, what we have looked at and touched with our hands, concerning the Word of life—and the life was manifested, and we have seen and testify and proclaim to you the eternal life, which was with the Father and was manifested to us—what we have seen and heard we proclaim to you also. (1 John 1:1–3)

We have a reliable collection of historical documents that were written by the men who lived through the events they recorded. They weren't like so many others, who claim they had a vision and wrote down everything they could remember. The apostles saw Christ with their own eyes, heard Him teach with their own ears, and touched Him with their own hands. The same is true of the Old Testament writers; they were eyewitnesses to the events they wrote about. The authors of Scripture experienced these things firsthand—or, as in Luke's case, they got the story directly from those who did.

VERIFIABLE CLAIMS

While it is important that the Bible was written by eyewitnesses, it's equally important that it was written *during the lifetime of other eyewitnesses*. Consider the statement Paul makes in 1 Corinthians regarding the witnesses to the risen Christ.

> Now I make known to you, brethren, the gospel which I preached to you, which also you received, in which also you stand, by which also you are saved, if you hold fast the word which I preached to you, unless you believed in vain. For I delivered to you as of first importance what I also received, that Christ died for our sins according to the Scriptures, and that He was buried, and that He was raised on the third day according to the Scriptures, and that He appeared to Cephas, then to the twelve. After that He appeared to more than five hundred brethren at one time, most of whom remain until now, but some have fallen asleep; then He appeared to James, then to all the apostles; and last of all, as to one untimely born, He appeared to me also. (1 Cor. 15:1–8)

Paul's point is that the resurrection wasn't a secret. Hundreds of people saw Christ after He rose from the grave, including many who were still alive when he wrote his first epistle to the Corinthians. Why is that important? It means the gospel was verifiable: The claim that Christ had risen from the dead could be tested. Paul's words could be disproven, but they never were.

The Word of God is harmonious in that regard. It does not disagree with itself. The accounts of one author are not undermined by the words of another. Nor are they, for that matter, by external evidence. There have been more than twenty-five thousand archeological digs directly related to the subject matter of the Bible. Not one of them has uncovered anything that has disproved or contradicted Scripture's claims. In fact, the overwhelming majority of them have confirmed the biblical account. That internal and external evidence demands to be weighed.

However, skeptics attempt to discount or dismiss that fact. They will argue that the Bible was written later—that it was assembled under the emperor Constantine, cobbled together from fragments handed down through history. Others point out that we don't have the original manuscripts of the biblical texts, and presume that the copies we do posses have been altered or amended.

And while it's true that we don't have the originals, we can get pretty close to them. We have manuscripts that date from between AD 100 and AD 120—that's within a couple decades of the completion of the New Testament. Moreover, we don't just have a few ancient texts to work with. For the New Testament alone, we have more than six thousand manuscripts or portions of manuscripts. And with them, we can trace the consistent message of the New Testament back to within a few decades of the last writings.

If that doesn't sound impressive to you, it's because you don't deal with ancient texts. Consider some examples: We have less than a dozen ancient manuscripts of Aristotle's *Poetics*, and the oldest one is from more than a thousand years after the original's composition. The same is true for Julius Caesar's *Gallic Wars*. On the other hand, we have hundreds of ancient copies of Homer's *Iliad*, but the oldest one was transcribed more than two thousand years after the original was written. And yet, people still have the audacity to question the reliability of the New Testament. No other ancient document comes close to the Bible in this regard, and if the Bible cannot be considered reliable, then certainly no ancient document can be.

Others try to skirt the wealth of documentation by arguing that all it would take is one overzealous scribe or monk to alter the Bible forever. But again, there are some obvious flaws with that theory. To begin with, there is the manuscript problem. Any monk or group of monks looking to alter the record of Scripture would have had to make changes to all the six thousand manuscripts and portions of manuscripts we currently possess, plus all the others that existed at the time. We're talking about a massive undertaking, requiring a multitude of agents working on a global scale in total secrecy and achieving a one hundred percent success rate. And not only would they have had to change all six thousand manuscripts, they would have had to change them in exactly the same way.

If that's not a large enough obstacle for the theory to overcome, let's also consider the language problem. The message of the gospel exploded out of Jerusalem at Pentecost. The Roman persecution spread believers even farther, carrying the truth about Christ to new cultures throughout the known world. Before long, the New Testament was translated into Syriac, Coptic, and Latin. And those manuscripts would have to match with all the other ones the overzealous monks altered. Which means they had to be able to lie in Syriac, Coptic, and Latin as well as they lied in Greek, all while keeping it completely secret from the rest of the world.

Finally, there is also the problem of the church fathers, who had a habit of quoting from and writing commentaries on the New Testament. In fact, if all we had were the writings of the church fathers, we would be able to reassemble all but eleven verses of the New Testament. Which means the overzealous monks, after finding and altering more than six thousand manuscripts, and convincingly sowing those same lies into the Syriac, Coptic, and Latin manuscripts, also had to find and amend all the works by all the church fathers, make sure all the lies matched up, and then return those works without anyone finding out what they had done.

It's safe to say the overzealous-monk theory is absolute fantasy.

I'll mention one other objection I often encounter with people attempting to dismiss the reliability and historicity of the Bible. You have likely heard someone claim that they can't believe the Bible because it has been translated so many times. What they're saying is that God's Word has lost the true intent of its message over time. Like an ancient game of Telephone, we can't possibly know what it originally said, much less meant.

It bothers me a great deal that there are people who claim to be educated and intelligent that continue to put forward this argument. It bothers me that Christians don't laugh them out of the room. To put it simply, the people who make this argument are either ignorant, or evil, or both.

Nobody really believes that Bible translation actually resembles a game of Telephone, with the message slowly diluted and lost over time. Bible translators don't simply work off the most recent previous translation—they go back to the original languages. And if you bother to learn those languages, you can check your translation against the originals. Or you can simply invest in software that will do it for you. In fact, it has never been easier to thoroughly test modern translations against the documents they claim to translate. With the translation capabilities we have today, there is nowhere to hide inaccuracies or illegitimate insertions.

Such foolish objections to the trustworthiness of Scripture are really just attempts to circumvent the fact that the Bible was written by eyewitnesses during the lifetime of other eyewitnesses. Rebellious hearts concoct fantasies and excuses to cloud the issue and distract from the reality that the potentially falsifiable claims in Scripture were never falsified.

MIRACULOUS WORKS

In explaining why we believe the Bible, so far we can firmly say that it is a reliable collection of historical documents written by eyewitnesses during the lifetime of other eyewitnesses. All of that is incredibly important, but if we stop there, all we have is a quality history book. We need to add an important clarification: that these eyewitnesses *report supernatural events*.

Peter picks up with the same idea back in our passage. "For when He received honor and glory from God the Father, such an utterance as this was made to Him by the Majestic Glory, 'This is My beloved Son with whom I am well-pleased'—and we ourselves heard this utterance made from heaven when we were with Him on the holy mountain" (2 Pet. 1:17–18).

We're not talking about superhuman events. These weren't mere feats of strength and athletic skill. These are *supernatural* events, like the Transfiguration of Jesus Christ. Here's how Mark's gospel records that miraculous event:

> Six days later, Jesus took with Him Peter and James and John, and brought them up on a high mountain by themselves. And He was transfigured before them; and His garments became

> radiant and exceedingly white, as no launderer on earth can whiten them. Elijah appeared to them along with Moses; and they were talking with Jesus. Peter said to Jesus, "Rabbi, it is good for us to be here; let us make three tabernacles, one for You, and one for Moses, and one for Elijah." For he did not know what to answer; for they became terrified. Then a cloud formed, overshadowing them, and a voice came out of the cloud, "This is My beloved Son, listen to Him!" All at once they looked around and saw no one with them anymore, except Jesus alone. (Mark 9:2–8)

The disciples were understandably amazed because nothing like that had ever happened before, nor would it happen again. Not only were they face-to-face with Elijah and Moses, they also saw a brief glimpse of Christ in His glorified majesty. Peter was so shocked that he impetuously offered to set up camp on the spot.

When we're defending the truth of Scripture, we need to remember that the Bible is not just a bunch of rules about religion. God's Word gives us a record of His miraculous work. It tells us in detail how He has revealed His character and nature through supernatural events, and how He miraculously protects and provides for His people. The Bible tells us how God delivered Israel out of Egypt and how He faithfully met their needs in the wilderness. It also tells us how He displayed His deity by healing the sick, how He endured the punishment for the sins of those who believe, and how He rose from the grave three days later. This is not merely the writings of a religious community trying to hand down their rules and regulations. Scripture is the record of God's supernatural work on behalf of His people.

FULFILLED PROPHECY

Not only does the Bible recount God's miraculous works, it shows us that these events *took place in fulfillment of specific prophecies*. As Peter writes, "So we have the prophetic word made more sure, to which you do well to pay attention as to a lamp shining in a dark place, until the day dawns and the morning star arises in your hearts" (2 Pet. 1:19). The fulfillment of biblical prophecy on its own won't save anyone, but each instance points to the truth about the Savior. Peter exhorts his readers to fix their eyes on the light revealed by fulfilled prophecy until the light of the gospel of Jesus Christ finally dawns in their hearts.

The kind of prophecy in mind here is not the general prediction of future events, as Nostradamus did. Nor are we talking about the vague prophecies of faith healers and charlatans. When you know enough about the human condition, it is easy to make broad assumptions about a large group of people. Inevitably, someone is suffering from back pain, while someone else likely lost his job. Platitudes and parlor tricks like that are not what we have in view when it comes to the fulfilled prophecy of Scripture.

Instead, we're dealing with undeniable specifics delivered sometimes hundreds of years before their fulfillment. This is true of passages like Isaiah 53, which was written over seven hundred years before the birth of Christ, predicting in detail how He would die as the suffering servant. While Jewish reading calendars include Isaiah 52 and Isaiah 54, chapter 53 is left out because it speaks with such undeniable specificity that it can't be referring to anyone but Christ. It leaves no room to conclude anything other than that Jesus is the fulfillment of that prophecy and that He is the long-awaited Messiah.

But maybe seven hundred years isn't quite impressive enough. Maybe we need to look to Psalm 22, which was written by David more than a thousand years before the life of Christ. Of course, that particular psalm has only been known by its chapter number for a few hundred years. Prior to that, it would have been known by its first line, which is, "My God, my God, why have You forsaken me?" (Ps. 22:1).

You and I recognize those words as the ones spoken by Christ in His final, agonizing moments on the cross. But to a first-century Jew standing within earshot of the dying Jesus, that was the first line of Psalm 22. And like most song lyrics, the first line brings to mind of the subsequent lines. For example, if I were to say to you, "Amazing grace, how sweet the sound," the next words in your mind would likely be, "That saved a wretch like me." And if I were to quote those words to you as I was about to be executed, you would likely think about the rest of the song the whole time I was dying.

In this case, the words of the song pointed to the event that was unfolding at that very moment. Those who heard the plea of Christ likely had their minds drawn to the words of Psalm 22 that were being fulfilled before their eyes. The scene played out before them exactly as David had written more than a thousand years prior. "Far from my deliverance are the words of my groaning. O my God, I cry by day, but You do not answer; and by night, but I have no rest" (vv. 1–2). David prophesied how Christ would suffer the scorn of the crowd—even down to some of the very insults they would hurl at Him. "But I am a worm and not a man, a reproach of men and despised by the people. All who see me sneer at me; they separate with the lip, they wag the head, saying, 'Commit yourself to the Lord; let Him deliver him; let Him rescue him, because He delights in him'" (vv. 6–8).

David continues, "Many bulls have surrounded me; strong bulls of Bashan have encircled me. They open wide their mouth at me, as a ravening and a roaring lion. I am poured out like water, and all my bones are out of joint; my heart is like wax; it is melted within me" (vv. 12–14). Nailed to the cross, Jesus would have been slumped and contorted. And after He died, they pierced His side, thrusting upward through the pericardium, spilling blood and water out of the wound (cf. John 19:34). There's more: "My strength is dried up like a potsherd, and my tongue cleaves to my jaws; and You lay me in the dust of death. For dogs have surrounded me; a band of evildoers has encompassed me; they pierced my hands and my feet. I can count all my bones. They look, they stare at me; they divide my garments among them, and for my clothing they cast lots" (Ps. 22:15–18). We know Jesus requested a drink while on the cross, only to receive a sponge full of sour wine (John 19:28–29). We know that none of His bones were broken in the process of His execution (vv. 31–37). And we know that He was surrounded by Roman soldiers who callously gambled for His clothes while He was still dying (vv. 23–25).

All of that horrifying detail was spelled out in the pages of Scripture more than a thousand years before the life of Christ, by a man who would never have seen a crucifixion with his own eyes. How do I know that? Because crucifixion had not been invented during David's lifetime.

The Bible speaks with a prophetic specificity that could only be divinely revealed. There is no other explanation for such vivid details spelled out centuries before they would come to pass.

DIVINELY AUTHORED

Finally, we need to recognize that the authors of Scripture *claim that their writings are divine, rather than human, in origin.* Peter writes, "But know this first of all, that no prophecy of Scripture is a matter of one's own interpretation, for no prophecy was ever made by an act of human will, but men moved by the Holy Spirit spoke from God" (2 Pet. 1:20–21). Paul said, "All Scripture is breathed out by God" (2 Tim. 3:16, ESV). Over and over, the testimony of the Bible is, "Thus sayeth the Lord." The Lord spoke to Moses. He spoke to Daniel, Isaiah, and Jeremiah. And through the Holy Spirit, He spoke to the apostles. Scripture is the record of what He said to them, and through them to us. They consistently point back to Him as the author of the Bible.

In an effort to avoid Scripture's divine authorship, some people will attempt the seemingly clever gambit of claiming they need scientific proof if they're going to believe the Bible is God's Word. While the "man of science" dodge might make some feel intellectual, it really only demonstrates their ignorance. They fail to understand that the scientific method they profess to revere only applies to events that are observable, measureable, and repeatable. History is none of those things. So saying you require scientific evidence to believe historical events only shows that a person doesn't know what he or she is talking about.

You don't use the scientific method to prove historical facts; you use the evidentiary method, like you would in a courtroom. You ask about the reliability of the sources, and if they can be corroborated. You ask about the internal and external evidence that supports the sources. You ask about the quality of the witnesses—were they trustworthy, and could their statements have been falsified? What is there that can contradict or confirm those statements?

Those are the kinds of questions you ask in the evidentiary method. And when you ask those questions, you come away with things like three continents, three languages, over forty authors, most of whom never met one another. They wrote sixty-six volumes, addressing hundreds of different subjects and topics, yet coming together in a cohesive unit that tells one redemptive story, although it was written over a period of more than fifteen hundred years. You have the corroboration of twenty-five thousand archeological digs related directly to matters discussed in the Bible that have only further confirmed the accuracy of the biblical record. And you have the writings of contemporaries that further confirm the details therein.

Looking at that enormous body of evidence, only a fool would say, "I simply can't believe the Bible is true."

On the other hand, the wise man says, "I choose to believe the Bible because it's a reliable collection of historical documents written by eyewitnesses during the lifetime of other eyewitnesses. They report supernatural events that took place in fulfillment of specific prophecies, and they claim that their writings are divine, rather than human, in origin."

And if that's not convincing enough, tell them you tried it, and it changed your life.

No.3

THE FINDING OF AN OLD BOOK

BY DR. JACK MACARTHUR

I'd like you to turn in your Bibles, if you will, to the second book of Kings. And actually, if I were to read the Scripture that I would like to read to you this morning, I would read the entire twenty-second chapter of 2 Kings, and then I would read chapters 34 and 35 of 2 Chronicles. And believe me, it might be more blessed and more meaningful if I just did that instead of preaching. But to save time this morning, I want you to look at verses 8–10, and then I'll build in the rest of the story for you.

> And Hilkiah the high priest said unto Shaphan the scribe, I have found the book of the law in the house of the Lord. And Hilkiah gave the book to Shaphan, and he read it. And Shaphan the scribe came to the king, and brought the king word again, and said, Thy servants have gathered the money that was found in the house, and have delivered it into the hand of them that do the work, that have the oversight of the house of the Lord.

> And Shaphan the scribe shewed the king, saying, Hilkiah the priest hath delivered me a book. And Shaphan read it before the king. (2 Kings 22:8–10)[1]

Now would you turn over to chapter 23, and just look at verse 3. "And the king stood by a pillar, and made a covenant before the Lord, to walk after the Lord, and to keep his commandments and his testimonies and his statutes with all their heart and all their soul, to perform the words of this covenant that were written in this book. And all the people stood to the covenant." Now keep your Bible handy, because you're going to need it.

THE YOUNG KING AND THE GREAT REVIVAL

I suppose in the roll call of all of the kings of Israel and Judah, there is no more wonderful name that could be read than the name of King Josiah. Interestingly, he came to the throne when he was only eight years of age, and he came at a time when apostasy and spiritual decline were widely evident. The people had gotten so far away from God that they were engaged in the practices of heathen religions. The Temple at Jerusalem had been hideously desecrated. Actually, ugly, gruesome altars to heathen idols were erected in the place where only God should be worshiped. Strangely and enigmatically, the sanctuary became a place of merchandise, of making money. Throughout the land, pagan altars had been built on the high places. And as you know, the study of archaeology has confirmed some of the ghastly practices of those who worshiped the goddesses of fertility—these terrible, immoral, perverted rites.

Think of it. The people who had once known the true God, historically, were caught in this horrible swill. Astrologers, fortune-tellers, and mediums flourished throughout the land. Israel had forgotten God and pushed His revealed will to one side.

---

[1] Unless otherwise noted, Scripture quotations in this chapter are from the King James Version.

The Word of God tells us that at the age of sixteen, Josiah was converted. In fact, in 2 Chronicles 34:3 we read that he began to seek after the God of his fathers. And soon after he found the Lord in this dynamic, life-changing experience, he instituted national reform. In 2 Chronicles 34–35 and 2 Kings 22–23, we read about the great and glorious changes he brought to the nation Israel. The high places with their graven images were removed. The altars of Baal were broken down. The terrible, immoral practices came to an end. And to symbolize the sincerity of his repentance, the bones of pagan priests were taken out of their sepulchers, where they had been buried with great honor, and instead they were burned on their own defiled altars.

In the eighteenth year of this wonderful young king's reign, he gave orders for the repairing of the Temple, and the work began with tremendous energy and desire. And the incident that I'm concerned with this morning, that we're going to use as a kind of a starting place, occurred at this particular time.

It seems that Hilkiah the high priest, while rummaging through the debris of the Temple, found a dust-covered scroll. And you will remember that those probably were huge. This particular scroll bore the title *The Book of the Law by the Hand of Moses*, and that would be the first five books—Genesis, Exodus, Leviticus, Numbers, and Deuteronomy. It would be what we call the Pentateuch. Hilkiah excitedly took the huge scroll that contained the Pentateuch to Shaphan the prime minister under Josiah—he was also the scribe. And he immediately recognized that it was the long-lost, neglected copy of the Scriptures, which had been, interestingly, originally deposited in the Ark of the Covenant and which had been used in the Temple for worship.

So this discovery was reported to the king, who immediately had the book read before him. And as the book was being read and he had the privilege of hearing the review of God's dealings with Israel, his heart was broken in sorrow and contrition, which led him to a renewal of his covenant vows. And he began to press his reforms to bring Israel back into a meaningful relationship with

God with renewed vigor. Concerning the days that followed, we read in 2 Chronicles 34:33, "And all his days [the people] departed not from following the Lord, the God of their fathers." What a beautiful testimony concerning the penetrating, powerful influence of this wonderful king.

Now there was not any question in the mind of King Josiah as to the authority, the authenticity, the integrity, or the inspiration of the Scriptures. But when he heard what God demanded of His people and then contrasted their repeated, protracted excursions into the horrible, idolatrous practices of these terrible religions, he tore his garments in distress and ordered that the rediscovered Word of God be read to all the people. My, what an interesting story this is.

I wonder if we ever, as I say so frequently, fall into a deadening familiarity with spiritual truth. I wonder how much the Word of God really means to us. Is it still an absolute, inerrant guide? Or perhaps those who've been exposed to a malignant atmosphere in which the authority of Scripture has been denied are now suffering under the stress of lacking confidence.

There never has been a time when the integrity and the authority of the Word of God has suffered more at the hands of erstwhile theologians than today. Of course, it disturbs me greatly. Theories of biblical inspiration range all the way from an extreme liberalism that rejects, entirely, infallible revelation and reduces the whole expression of Scripture to mythology, to the vagaries of enigmatic neo-orthodoxy, that equates the Scriptures with some kind of a mysticism, promoting a definition of inspiration that becomes absolutely incomprehensible.

I have said this to you so many times in our series on the facts and the mysteries of the Christian faith, but if the Bible is to maintain its integrity and authority, then we must never depart one hair's breadth from the position of absolute fidelity to the Scriptures as God's infallible Word. Literal, plenary inspiration—we believe that the original documents were given exactly as God would give them, and that they were absolutely pure. As you know, I'm a great champion for the verbal inspiration of the holy Book—that every word written was written under the divine direction of the Holy Spirit. And I believe that 2 Peter 1:21 explodes forever the idea that man has anything to do with inspiration; it's all the marvelous work of the Holy Spirit. For, as Peter tells us, "No prophecy was ever made by an act of human will, but men moved by the Holy Spirit spoke from God" (NASB).

Now the Bible is not lost to the world, because the promise in it says that the Word of our God endures forever. Our Lord said, "Heaven and earth shall pass away, but my words shall not pass away" (Matt. 24:35; cf. Mark 13:31; Luke 21:33). And no matter how titanic or no matter how universal the effort may seem to depreciate and destroy it, it can't be done. The Word of God is indestructible. But for all intents and purposes, it is indeed lost to the man who no longer believes in its divine inspiration. Or, for that matter, the revelation of God is lost to the man who does not love it. What a serious thing it is to lose the Word of God.

When we do lose it, to use some of the metaphors of Scripture, we lose God's mirror, that enables us to see ourselves as we really are. We lose God's lamp, or light, to show us the direction we should go. We lose God's milk to nourish our souls, and we lose God's water to quench our thirst. We lose God's mold, by which our lives are to be shaped.

THE DEVIL'S DELIGHT

The adversary of our souls delights when the Word of God becomes lost, because he hates it. He hates it, first of all, because it's powerful. Oh, what penetrating power there is in the Word of God. Take a look at that glorious Scripture once again in the fourth chapter of Hebrews, verse 12, "For the word of God is quick, and powerful, and sharper than any twoedged sword, piercing even to the dividing asunder of soul and spirit, and of the joints and marrow, and is a discerner of the thoughts and intents of the heart." My, there is something so mysterious about the power of the Word of God. It's difficult for me not to just start to preach a message on the power of the Word!

Furthermore, Satan hates the Word of God because it is pure. As I was thinking about this last night, I was thinking of several scriptures. Turn to the book of Proverbs just a moment, and look at chapter 30 verse 5. Notice what it says: "Every word of God is pure: he is a shield unto them that put their trust in him." Turn very quickly to Psalm 12:6, "The words of the Lord are pure words: as silver tried in a furnace of earth, purified seven times." Look at Psalm 19:8, "The statutes of the Lord are right, rejoicing the heart: the commandment of the Lord is pure, enlightening the eyes." And then those words found way over in the little book of James, chapter 3 verse 17, "But the wisdom that is from above is first pure, then peaceable, gentle, and easy to be intreated, full of mercy and good fruits, without partiality, and without hypocrisy."

The Word of God is *pure*. My, what an exciting thought that is. It is not contaminated; it is not polluted. It is as pure as the mind and the heart of God. It's pure truth. We always remember how Pilate said to Jesus in philosophical dilemma, "What is truth?" (John 18:38). What was he saying? He was saying, "Oh, how difficult it is to ever find out the truth about anything." Because even if you get some truth, there's some contamination in it; it isn't *pure* truth. The Word of God as given by the Spirit of God to the men who wrote the Scriptures was absolutely pure.

And then because it's pure, Satan also hates the Word of God because it's precious. Oh, how infinitely precious the Word of God is! Second Peter 1:4, "Whereby are given unto us exceeding great and precious promises: that by these ye might be partakers of the divine nature, having escaped the corruption that is in the world through lust." We could talk about this for a long time. How precious is the Word of God. I think about the fact that I have the privilege of having something like four thousand volumes in my library. As all of you know by now, I am a book lover. But I would trade that whole library off in five minutes if I had to make a choice between those four thousand books and this book. This is *the* Book.

Oh, how precious it is.

Satan also hates the Word of God because it purges, it cleanses. You get in the Word of God, and the Spirit of God applies the Word of God to your life, and all of a sudden your life begins to be marvelously purified. What did our Lord say in John 15:3? "You are already clean because of the word which I have spoken to you" (NASB). Notice also the beautiful words of our Lord concerning the church in Ephesians 5. This is actually an exalted expression of what happens when we are Spirit-filled. In verse 18, we're urged to be filled with the Spirit, and then from that point on, all the way through the ninth verse of chapter 6, we're seeing the glorious results of being filled with the Spirit. In particular, Ephesians 5:25–26, in that marvelous passage on Christian marriage, highlights the purging power of the Word. "Husbands, love your wives, even as Christ also loved the church, and gave himself for it; that he might sanctify and cleanse it with the washing of water by the word." When we sit under the preaching and the teaching of the Word of God, it begins to filter through your life. Oh, what a purging power it has!

We also know that Satan hates the Word of God because it inevitably brings blessing. When you get in the Word and the Word begins to get in you, you inevitably receive God's blessings. Our minds are drawn to the beautiful words of Psalm 1.

> Blessed is the man that walketh not in the counsel of the ungodly, nor standeth in the way of sinners, nor sitteth in the seat of the scornful. But his delight is in the law of the Lord; and in his law doth he meditate day and night. And he shall be like a tree planted by the rivers of water, that bringeth forth his fruit in his season; his leaf also shall not wither; and whatsoever he doeth shall prosper. (Ps. 1:1–3)

God uses His Word to richly and abundantly bless His people.

Along those same lines, Satan hates the Word of God because it's filled with promises. Somebody took the time to count all the promises to believers in Scripture, and came up with a total of thirty thousand. And they aren't like the promises of a politician. God's promises to His people are always "Yea and amen!" God's Word is always true, and His promises are sure.

Finally, Satan hates the Word of God because it pronounces his doom. Our adversary knows his end has already been determined. And he wants to draw God's Word into question because it spells out his ultimate defeat.

That's why he takes great delight when the Bible is lost. He hates it, and he wants us to ignore and dismiss it.

HOW TO LOSE THE BIBLE

Let's turn our attention back to 2 Kings. Now this particular copy of the Scriptures that Hilkiah found and gave to Shaphan, and Shaphan gave to King Josiah—it's interesting how it got lost. Some think that it was through carelessness. Others think that it was laid away, and laid away with such care that it was forgotten. Have you ever done that? I have. You have something that you really wanted to save, and so you put it away and then forget where you put it. Others feel that it was maliciously hidden, that somebody hid it so that nobody would find it. And there are some who argue that it was laid away for safekeeping, so that no enemy would get it.

Let me ask you something—have you lost your Bible? You can lose your Bible. I'm not referring to the printed copy that you possess. The Bible can be lost, first of all, by neglect. It's possible to lose it this way while you still have it in your pocket. I'm confident that there isn't anyone in this congregation this morning that doesn't have a copy of the Word of God, perhaps many copies. I'm not sure, however, that all of us are reading the Word as we ought. And a Bible that isn't read is a lost Bible.

Whenever you neglect the Word of God and the application of its truth by the Spirit of God to your heart and your life, two things happen. First, you become ignorant as to its content. Many professing Christians live more in the newspaper, novels, and secular periodicals than they do in the Bible. Many are far more interested in the parade of passing sports or current events than they are in the mighty, tremendous revelation of God's eternal truth. And through the years of my ministry, as I've preached in conferences and meetings and churches all over the United States, Canada, and even Europe, I've never gotten over the shock of the abysmal ignorance of most professing Christians with respect to the Word of God. The ignorance of people with respect to the content of the Word of God is shocking.

I recently read about a test on the Bible, given by a teacher in Massachusetts to high school upperclassmen. Over eighty percent of the students could not complete the quote, "The love of money is the root of _____." They didn't know what to put in the blank. Others thought Sodom and Gomorrah were two lovers in the Old Testament. A great many students said that the gospels were written by Matthew, Mark, *Luther*, and John. And what I thought was one of the most interesting remarks—one student wrote on his paper that Eve was made out of an apple. The teacher was using the test to advance the idea that the Bible ought to be taught in schools, because the knowledge of Scripture is necessary due to all the biblical allusions found in literature, music, and the arts. And he said if our young people don't know anything about the Bible, they are going to be very ignorant when it comes to so much of the fine arts.

If there is an appalling ignorance on the part of those who are *outside* the church, far too many within the church are just as hopelessly ignorant of the treasures of the Word of God. The real responsibility and ministry of the church of Jesus Christ is to preach and teach the Word of God. Too many times, people are on a diet of topical preaching, like I'm doing this morning. This is topical preaching, and there is a reason why I don't do much of this. Because with topical preaching, you might be encouraged and admonished, but the way you truly feed people is you take book after book and you teach, teach, teach.

I remember the night I came home and walked into the bedroom where my mother and father were, and I said to my father, "You know, Dad, I feel that God wants me to be a minister." And he said, "Jack, that's something that your mother and I have prayed for, and I'm so glad about that." And then he gave me a Bible. And it's worn out and long gone now, but what he wrote in the front of it is not worn out and long gone. This was the challenge that he laid upon my heart:

> I charge thee therefore before God, and the Lord Jesus Christ, who shall judge the quick and the dead at his appearing and his kingdom; preach the word; be [diligent] in season, out of season; reprove, rebuke, exhort with all longsuffering and doctrine. For the time will come when they will not endure sound doctrine; but after their own lusts shall they heap to themselves teachers, having itching ears; and they shall turn away their ears from the truth, and shall be turned unto fables. But watch thou in all things, endure afflictions, do the work of an evangelist, make full proof of thy ministry. (2 Tim. 4:1–5)

That was my father's charge to me, but it was also God's charge. Oh, how necessary it is, beloved, that we saturate ourselves with the Word of God! And I want to warn you about something. Getting ten people together and getting out a Bible and reading a verse and saying, "Now what do *you* think it means? And what do *you* think it means?"—that is not studying the Bible. If you're going to study the Word, you need to get somebody who knows something about it to teach you. Like Paul says, "How shall they hear without a preacher?" (Rom. 10:14). He charged Timothy, "Study to shew thyself approved unto God, a workman that needeth not to be ashamed, rightly dividing the word of truth" (2 Tim. 2:15). There isn't anything that is more enhancing to your Christian life and to the edification of the Body than the careful study of the Word of God.

And you know, I have a great many dreams, and I never give up. My dream is that we'll see this church filled on Wednesday nights for the teaching of the Word of God. That we'll fill both our services on Sunday mornings. By the way, Johnny's church is going to three services on Sunday morning starting in September. That means he'll have three thousand there for their morning service. We certainly thank the Lord for the love of the Word that's generated in the hearts of those people. When you begin to love the Word of God, then wonderful things begin to happen, glorious things. So we need to know the Word.

The tragic fruit of neglecting the Word of God is not just ignorance; the second tragedy is a barren life. And not just barren, but a powerless and dissatisfied life is inevitable when you neglect the Bible habit of the Christian life, of reading the Word of God. And today we're living in a time when people want everything the easy way. You used to have to percolate coffee; you don't have to do that anymore. You can just stick the spoon in the jar and slap it in the hot water and give it one stir, and you've got coffee. In the same way people today are seeking spiritual shortcuts. Instead of faithfully studying and seeking a true knowledge of the Word of God, they pursue some kind of an experience that will just shortcut the whole thing. That is the way the Charismatic movement is going.

D. L. Moody said many years ago that he never saw a useful Christian who was not a student of the Word of God. You likely remember the old saying, "These have God married, and no man shall part, dust on the Bible and drought in the heart." Dr. Keith Brooks said the Bible is like some people, it's shy and retiring. Buy one, and in three days you can't find it. It gets covered with newspapers or hidden behind the Sears Roebuck catalog or some magazine. You can, however, overcome its shyness by making it feel at home and by giving it regular recognition, by courting it in your spare moments, and in this you will be well repaid. Salmasius, one of the greatest scholars in his time, when he was dying, instructed those who were standing around his bedside to "mind the world less and God more." And I always remember how Patrick Henry, when he was dying, said, "My greatest regret is that I could never find time to read the Bible, and now it is too late." We lose the Bible when we neglect it.

We also lose our Bible by reading it superficially. In John 5:39, our Lord gave the scribes and Pharisees a backhanded compliment when He said, "You search the Scriptures" (NASB). The Greek word translated "search" speaks of an earnest quest for hidden treasure. That is how we're meant to study the Word of God—thoroughly and intensely.

A man may run fleet-footed for a time over the richest gold fields and not even know they're there. If he would find the precious metal, it's because he digs. Much of our Bible reading is profitless because we are not reading it in earnest. Too often we read in a hurried way, scarcely pausing to reflect. Over time, our reading becomes perfunctory. Others read it out of a sense of duty, rather than searching it for the truth to edify and bless our souls. We can easily lose our Bible if we fail to read it thoughtfully and prayerfully.

Third, we can lose our Bibles by studying *about* them rather reading them. Now this may seem paradoxical, but it's an absolute fact. You can study the structure of the Bible, the chronology of the Bible, the geography of the Bible, the history of the Bible; you can listen to a series of messages like I'm bringing on the facts and the mysteries of the Christian faith; and that's all good. But you still haven't gotten into the message of the Bible. You're authenticating it, but you're not getting to the message. One of the criticisms of many of our modern seminaries is the fact that they spend most of their time in a critical analysis of the Bible: examining to see whether Moses really did write the Pentateuch, and whether there is one Isaiah or two. And when these men leave seminary, many times they have a very, very fine knowledge of what we call higher criticism and how to meet it and answer it. But many times they don't know what's in the Book.

I suppose the best illustration would be if you got a letter from a friend, yet you never bothered to read the letter. Instead you examined the envelope, and you measured how long it was and how wide it was. And then maybe you tested the glue, and then you analyzed what was in the glue. And then you looked at the stamp, and you thought it was a very interesting stamp, and so you gradually steamed the stamp off and you put that in your collection. And then you tried to find out what kind of paper that they used, and where the paper might have come from, of whether it was a pulp paper made from wood or whether it came from rags. And oh, you could have a great time. But what did the person send the letter to you for? What was the purpose of the letter? That you might read and study the *contents*. Normally, when we get a letter, we don't pay much attention to anything but getting it open and getting to the message. And that's the way you ought to approach the Word of God: Get to the content. And the more erudite and the more academic the approach to the Scripture, frequently the less satisfaction there is for the soul. We must read the Bible as the literal bread of God for our spiritual nourishment and growth.

So we understand that the Bible is lost by neglect, and by reading without studying. There is a fourth way we lose our Bible—and this is probably most important of all—that is when it's not translated into action. We lose our Bible when we do not, under the empowerment of the Holy Spirit, *obey it*. God ceases to impart spiritual strength and blessing when we willfully disobey the truth that's made clear to us. We do well to remember that the Bible was not merely given to us for doctrine; it was given to regulate our conduct. The Word of God says it's not the hearer of the Word of God, but the *doer* of the Word who is justified in His sight.

A man boasted, for example, that he'd read the Old Testament through twenty-three times, and the New Testament thirty-seven times. But he was such a disagreeable old grouch that everybody stayed away from him. He had done a lot of reading, but it hadn't done anything to him. A man may know the Bible and be a learned theologian, and yet be a very miserable, unhappy man, and even an ungodly man. Many such men try to get hold of the Bible, without letting the Bible get hold of them. The fact is, the more a man knows about the holy Book, the less fortunate he is—unless it gets into the very nerve and the fiber of his being.

I see the time has gone; I've just introduced what I want to say to you. But turn with me for just a moment to the book of James.

> But be ye doers of the word, and not hearers only, deceiving your own selves. For if any be a hearer of the word, and not a doer, he is like unto a man beholding his natural face in a glass: For he beholdeth himself, and goeth his way, and straightaway forgetteth what manner of man he was. But whoso looketh into the perfect law of liberty, and continueth therein, he being not a forgetful hearer, but a doer of the work, *this man shall be blessed in his deed.* (Jas. 1:22–25, emphasis added)

Oh my, there's so many ways that we can lose the Word of God. We can lose it, number five, when we substitute something else in its place. Jesus said to the religious leaders of His day, "Ye made the commandment of God of none effect by your tradition" (Matt. 15:6). The scribes and Pharisees had overlaid the law of God with the teaching and traditions of the rabbis.

In the same way, some in our day substitute prayer books and the teaching of the church for the Bible itself. And there is a danger that some lean too heavily on lesson helps and commentaries that become a substitute for the study of Scripture. I do not mean to underestimate the use of study aids—I use them myself. But the danger is in allowing them to take the place of the Bible, to push the Word aside and wrongly occupy the focus of our study. We must remember that the Bible is a jealous book, and it tolerates no rivals. It stands alone and complete.

There's a sixth way we lose our Bible—we lose it by perversion. That is, we lose it by distorting it to suit our own prejudices, or by wresting it from its true meaning and twisting it to teach something that is false. Jeremiah 23:36 condemns the false prophets who had "perverted the words of the living God." In Acts 20:30, Paul issued a warning to the early church, saying, "Also of your own selves shall men arise, speaking perverse things, to draw away disciples after them." How many people have lost their Bibles because it's been perverted by some specious cult system? Oh, beware lest these perverters of the Word, through the substitution of their parallel writings and professed revelations, rob you of your Bible and its precious truth.

Along with the perversion of the Word, we could also say we lose our Bibles when it is mutilated. We are not at liberty to pick and choose among the Bible's teachings, for how shall we determine what to keep and what to let go? Shall we keep what we like and throw away what we do not like? Some are losing their Bibles by doing that very thing.

A liberal minister visited one of his dying members and asked this member if he'd like him to read something from the Bible, and the man said yes. And so the pastor asked the man's wife for his Bible. The dying man's wife brought a tattered, torn, mutilated Bible to him. Whole books had been torn out. Verses here and there had been cut out. And the minister said to her, "Is this the best Bible you've got?" The dying man answered, he said, "Yes, that's all that's left. When you came to our church, it was all there. But whenever you told us that certain books were not really the Word of God, I tore them out. Because I just wanted to see what would happen to my Bible. And when you said certain verses shouldn't be there, I took those out. And the fact is, if I'd listened to you much longer, I wouldn't have had anything left but the covers."

The Word of God is its own witness. And every portion and part rests on the same, identical authority. And on the basis of its claims, it is either all true, or it is not true at all. Don't forget that to reckon one section as inspired and another section not inspired is to rob the book of its inspiration altogether. Let us beware lest these mutilators of the Bible with their piecemeal theories of inspiration take the Bible from us.

Oh, the loss of the Bible is an inestimable loss! It's like the sun going out, leaving the soul enveloped in gloom and hopelessness.

RECOVERING WHAT HAD BEEN LOST

Well, how do you find your lost Bible? By doing exactly what

Josiah did. And I haven't got time to read it to you, but first of all, he heard it. He had Shaphan read it to him. He had Shaphan read the first five books of the Bible, right straight through, and he sat and heard every word. And then he began to use it, because he believed it. And then, he called the people for the reading of the Word of God, and he read it to them. And Scripture tells us the Spirit of God fell upon the people.

Not only did Josiah hear the Word, he also practiced it. We have the beautiful story in 2 Chronicles 34:33, "And Josiah took away all the abominations out of all the countries that pertained to the children of Israel, and made all that were present in Israel to serve, even to serve the Lord their God. And all his days they departed not from following the Lord, the God of their fathers." The result of finding God's Word was a revival—not only throughout the land, but also in Josiah's heart.

Oh listen, do you love the Word of God? There's no greater proof that you have really passed from death unto life than if you have an insatiable love for the Word of God. Some years ago, I read about an old gentleman who discovered five thousand dollars in a family Bible that had been left to him. Bank notes were scattered all through the book. Get this—many years earlier in 1874, this man's aunt died, and one clause of her will read, "To my beloved nephew, I will and bequeath my Bible, and all that it contains, with the residue of my estate after my financial expenses and just and lawful debts have been paid." Do you know how many years it was before he opened that Bible? *Thirty-five years*. And in that time he had suffered great financial troubles. He lived in poverty most of those years. And while he was packing his trunk in order to move in with his son and his son's wife, to live out the few remaining years of his life, he at last opened that old Bible, and then the notes began to fall out. What regret must have come to his mind, knowing that this rich treasure had lain idle for thirty-five years.

Our God has given us a costly treasure in His Word. In this Book of books are stored the riches of the wisdom and knowledge of God. All that we need spiritually is found in its pages.

Yet these riches, put at our disposal by a loving God, are, to a large extent, unknown and unused. Instead of being enjoyed, they are neglected. Many of us who claim to be Christians are dragging along in a spiritually impoverished state, when we might be living powerful, fruitful lives. May God help us to arise and possess our possessions in Him. May He give us the love for His Word that Jeremiah described: "Thy words were found, and I did eat them; and thy word was unto me the joy and rejoicing of mine heart: for I am called by thy name, O Lord God of hosts" (Jer. 15:16).

Is your Bible lost, friend? Oh, find it before it is too late!

No.4

THE SUFFICIENCY OF SCRIPTURE

BY JOHN MACARTHUR

As noted in the foreword, we took the liberty of including this previously published chapter from John MacArthur's book, The Inerrant Word, *without his knowledge. We believe it is the best discourse on the sufficiency of Scripture since the Puritan era, and a fitting addition to this volume. –Ed.*

Psalm 19 is the earliest biblical text that gives us a comprehensive statement on the superiority of Scripture. It categorically affirms the authority, inerrancy, and sufficiency of the written Word of God. It does this by comparing the truth of Scripture to the breathtaking grandeur of the universe, and it declares that the Bible is a better revelation of God than all the glory of the galaxies. Scripture, it proclaims, is perfect in every regard.

The psalm thereby sets Scripture above every other truth claim. It is a sweeping, definitive affirmation of the utter perfection and absolute trustworthiness of God's written Word. There is no more succinct summation of the power and precision of God's written Word anywhere in the Bible.

Psalm 19 is basically a condensed version of Psalm 119, the longest chapter in all of Scripture. Psalm 119 takes 176 verses to expound on the same truths Psalm 19 outlines in just eight verses (vv. 7–14).

Every Christian ought to affirm and fully embrace the same high view of Scripture the psalmist avows in Psalm 19. If we are going to live in obedience to God's Word—especially those who are called to teach the Scriptures—we need to do so with this confidence in mind.

After all, *faith* (not moralism, good works, vows, sacraments, or rituals, but *belief in Christ as He is revealed in Scripture*) is what makes a person a Christian. "Without faith it is impossible to please Him, for he who comes to God must believe that He is and that He is a rewarder of those who seek Him" (Heb. 11:6). "For by grace you have been saved through faith; and that not of yourselves, it is the gift of God; not as a result of works" (Eph. 2:8–9).

The only sure and safe ground of true faith is the Word of God (2 Pet. 1:19–21). It is "the message of truth, the gospel of [our] salvation" (Eph. 1:13). For a Christian to doubt the Word of God is the grossest kind of self-contradiction.

When I began in ministry nearly half a century ago, I fully expected I would need to deal with assaults against Scripture from unbelievers and worldlings. I was prepared for that. Unbelievers by definition reject the truth of Scripture and resist its authority. "The mind set on the flesh is hostile toward God; for it does not subject itself to the law of God, for it is not even able to do so" (Rom. 8:7).

But from the beginning of my ministry until today, I have witnessed—and have had to deal with—wave after wave of attacks against the Word of God coming *mostly from within the evangelical community*. Over the course of my ministry, virtually all the most dangerous assaults on Scripture I've seen have come from seminary professors, megachurch pastors, charismatic charlatans on television, popular evangelical authors, "Christian psychologists," and bloggers on the evangelical fringe. The evangelical movement has no shortage of theological tinkerers and self-styled apologists who seem to think the way to win the world is to embrace whatever theories are currently in vogue regarding evolution, morality, epistemology, or whatever—and then reframe our view of Scripture to fit this worldly "wisdom." The Bible is treated like Silly Putty, pressed and reshaped to suit the shifting interests of popular culture.

Of course, God's Word will withstand every attack on its veracity and authority. As Thomas Watson said, "The devil and his agents have been blowing at scripture light, but could never prevail to blow it out—a clear sign that it was lighted from heaven."[1] Nevertheless, Satan and his minions are persistent, seeking to derail believers whose faith is fragile, or dissuade unbelievers from even considering the claims of Scripture.

To make their attacks more subtle and effective, the forces of evil disguise themselves as angels of light and servants of righteousness (2 Cor. 11:13–15). That's why the most dangerous attacks on Scripture come from within the community of professing believers. They are relentless, and we need to be relentless in opposing them.

Over the years as I have confronted the various onslaughts of evangelical skepticism, I have returned to Psalm 19 again and again. It is a definitive answer to virtually every modern and postmodern attack on the Bible. It offers an antidote to the parade of faulty ministry philosophies and silly fads that so easily capture the fancy of today's evangelicals. It refutes the common misconception that science, psychology, and philosophy must be mastered and integrated with biblical truth in order to give the Bible more credibility. It holds the answer to what currently ails the visible church. It is a powerful testimony about the glory, power, relevance, clarity, efficacy, inerrancy, and sufficiency of Scripture.

I want to focus here on a passage in the second half of the psalm—just three verses, beginning with verse 7, that speak

[1] Thomas Watson, *A Body of Practical Divinity* (T. Wardle, 1833), 23.

specifically about the Scriptures.

This is a psalm of David, and in the opening six verses, he speaks of *general revelation*. As a young boy tending his father's sheep, he had plenty of time to gaze at the night sky and ponder the greatness and glory of God as revealed in nature. That's what he describes in the opening lines of the psalm: "The heavens are telling of the glory of God; and their expanse is declaring the work of His hands" (v. 1). Through creation, God reveals Himself at all times, across all language barriers, to all people and nations: "Day to day pours forth speech, and night to night reveals knowledge. There is no speech, nor are there words; their voice is not heard. Their line has gone out through all the earth, and their utterances to the end of the world" (vv. 2–4). God declares Himself in His creation day and night, unceasingly. The vastness of the universe, all the life it contains, and all the laws that keep it orderly rather than chaotic are a testimony to, and a manifestation of, the wisdom and glory of God.

As grand and glorious as creation is, however, we cannot discern all the spiritual truth we need to know from it. General revelation does not give a clear account of the gospel. Nature tells us nothing specific about Christ; His incarnation, death, and resurrection; the atonement He made for sin; the doctrine of justification by faith; or a host of other truths essential to salvation and eternal life.

Special revelation is the truth God has revealed in Scripture. That is the subject David takes up in the second half of the psalm, beginning in verse 7. Having extolled the vast glory of creation and the many marvelous ways it reveals truth about God, he turns now to Scripture and says the written Word of God is more pure, more powerful, more permanent, more effectual, more telling, more reliable, and *more glorious* than all the countless wonders written across the universe.

> The law of the Lord is perfect, restoring the soul;
> The testimony of the Lord is sure, making wise the simple.

> The precepts of the Lord are right, rejoicing the heart;
> The commandment of the Lord is pure, enlightening the eyes.
> The fear of the Lord is clean, enduring forever;
> The judgments of the Lord are true; they are righteous altogether.
> (Ps. 19:7–9)

In those three brief verses, David makes six statements—two in verse 7, two in verse 8, and two in verse 9. He uses six titles for Scripture: *law, testimony, precepts, commandment, fear*, and *judgments*. He lists six characteristics of Scripture: It is *perfect, sure, right, pure, clean,* and *true*. And he names six effects of Scripture on the human soul: It *restores the soul, makes wise the simple, rejoices the heart, enlightens the eyes, endures forever*, and *produces comprehensive righteousness*.

Thus, the Holy Spirit—with an astounding and supernatural economy of words—sums up everything that needs to be said about the power, sufficiency, comprehensiveness, and trustworthiness of Scripture.

Notice, first of all, that all six statements have the phrase "of the Lord"—just in case someone might question the source of Scripture. This is the law of the Lord—*His* testimony. These are the precepts and commandments of God Himself. The Bible is of divine origin. It is the inspired revelation of the Lord God.

By breaking these three couplets down and looking at each phrase, we can begin to gather a sense of the power and the greatness of Scripture. Again, the opening verses of the psalm were all about the vast glory revealed in creation. Thus, the central point of the whole psalm is that *the grandeur and glory of Scripture is infinitely greater than that of the entire created universe.*

GOD'S WORD IS PERFECT, REVIVING THE SOUL

That point is made powerfully yet simply in David's first statement about Scripture in verse 7: "The law of the Lord is perfect, restoring the soul." The Hebrew word translated as "law" is *torah*. To this day, Jews use the word *Torah* to refer to the Pentateuch (the five books penned by Moses). Those five books are, of course, the heart and the starting point of the Old Testament—but the psalms and prophets are likewise inspired Scripture, equally authoritative (cf. Luke 24:44). When David speaks of "the law of the Lord" in this context, he has the whole canon in mind. "The law," as the term is used here, refers not merely to the Ten Commandments; not just to the 613 commandments that constitute the *mitzvot* of Moses's law; not even to the Torah considered as a unit. He is using the word "law" as a figure of speech to signify all of Scripture.

Throughout Scripture, "the law" often refers to the entire canon. This kind of expression is called *synecdoche*, a figure of speech in which part of something is used to represent the whole. You find this same language in Joshua 1:8, for example. That verse famously speaks of "this book of the law"—meaning not just the commandments contained therein, but all of Scripture as it existed in Joshua's time—Genesis and Job as well as Leviticus and Deuteronomy. Psalm 119 repeatedly uses the same figure of speech (cf. vv. 1, 18, 29, 34, 44, etc.).

When used that way, the language stresses the didactic nature of God's Word. "Blessed is the man whom You chasten, O Lord, and whom You teach out of Your law" (Ps. 94:12). "Graciously teach me your law!" (Ps. 119:29, ESV). David is thinking of Scripture as a manual on righteous human behavior—*all* Scripture, not merely Moses's law. After all, "All Scripture is inspired by God and profitable for teaching, for reproof, for correction, for training in righteousness; so that the man of God may be adequate, equipped for every good work" (2 Tim. 3:16–17).

And all of Scripture is "*perfect.*" Many years ago, I researched that word as it appears in the Hebrew text. It's the Hebrew word *tamim*, which is variously translated in assorted English versions as "unblemished," "without defect," "whole," "blameless," with "integrity," "complete," "undefiled," or "perfect." I traced the Hebrew word through several lexicons to try to discern whether there might be some nuance or subtlety that would shade our understanding of it. I spent three or four hours looking up every use of that word in the biblical text. In the end it was clear: The word means "perfect." It is an exact equivalent of the English word in all its shades of meaning.

David is using the expression in an unqualified, comprehensive way. Scripture is superlative in every sense. Not only is it flawless, it is also sweeping and thorough. That's not to suggest that it contains everything that can possibly be known. Obviously, the Bible is not an encyclopedic source of information about every conceivable subject. But as God's instruction for man's life, it is perfect. It contains everything we need to know about God, His glory, faith, life, and the way of salvation. Scripture is not deficient or defective in any way. It is perfect in both its accuracy and its sufficiency.

In other words, it contains everything God has revealed for our spiritual instruction. It is the sole authority by which to judge anyone's creed (what he believes), character (what he is), or conduct (what the does).

More specifically, according to our text, Scripture is perfect in its ability to restore and transform the human soul. "For the word of God is living and active and sharper than any two-edged sword, and piercing as far as the division of soul and spirit, of both joints and marrow, and able to judge the thoughts and intentions of the heart" (Heb. 4:12). For believers, the piercing and soul work described in that verse is a wholly beneficial procedure, comparable to spiritual heart surgery. It is that process described in Ezekiel 36:26, where the Lord says, "I will give you a new heart and put a new spirit within you; and I will remove the heart of stone from your flesh and give you a heart of flesh." The instrument God uses in that process is the sword of the Spirit, which is Word of God. "Of His will He brought us forth *by the word of truth*" (Jas. 1:18, emphasis added). Jesus said, "The words that I have spoken to you are spirit and are life" (John 6:63). David acknowledges the life-giving principle of God's Word by saying, "The law of the Lord is perfect, restoring the soul" (Ps. 19:7).

In the Hebrew text, the word for "soul" is *nephesh*. As used here, the idea stands in contrast to the body. It speaks of the inner person. If you trace the Hebrew word *nephesh* through the Old Testament, you will find that in the best English versions of the Bible, it is translated in a dozen or more ways. It can mean "creature," "person," "being," "life," "mind," "self," "appetite," "desire," or "soul"—but it is normally used to signify the true person, the you that never dies.

So what is the statement saying? Scripture, in the hands of the Holy Spirit, can restore and regenerate someone who is dead in sin. Nothing else has that power—no manmade story, no clever carnal insight, no deep human philosophy. The Word of God is the only power that can totally transform the whole inner person.

GOD'S WORD IS TRUSTWORTHY, IMPARTING WISDOM

The second half of Psalm 19:7 turns the diamond slightly and looks at a different facet of Scripture: "The testimony of the Lord is sure, making wise the simple." Here Scripture is spoken of as God's self-revelation. A *testimony* is the personal account of a reliable witness. In everyday language, that word is normally reserved for formal, solemn statements from firsthand sources—usually either in legal or religious contexts. Eyewitnesses give sworn testimony in court. Believers relate how they came to faith, and we call that a testimony. The word conveys the idea of a formal declaration from a trustworthy source.

Scripture is God's testimony. This is God's own account of who He is and what He is like. It is God's self-disclosure. How wonderful that God has revealed Himself in such a grand and voluminous way—sixty-six books (thirty-nine in the Old Testament, twenty-seven in the New)—all revealing truth about God so that we may know Him and rest securely in the truth about Him.

"The testimony of the Lord is *sure*." That is its central characteristic. It is true. It is reliable. It is trustworthy.

The world is full of books you cannot trust. As a matter of

fact, any book written by man apart from the inspiration of the Holy Spirit will contain errors and deficiencies of various kinds. But the Word of the Lord is absolutely reliable. Every fact, every claim, every doctrine, and every statement of Scripture comes to us "not in words taught by human wisdom, but in those taught by the Spirit" (1 Cor. 2:13).

And what is the impact of this? Scripture "[makes] wise the simple" (Ps. 19:7). "Simple" is translated from a Hebrew expression that speaks of naive ignorance. It can be used as a disparaging term, describing people who are callow, gullible, or just silly. It's the same Hebrew word used in Proverbs 7:7, "I have seen among the simple, I have perceived among the youths, a young man lacking sense" (ESV); and 14:15, "The naive believes everything." The term signifies someone without knowledge or understanding.

But the derivation of the word suggests the problem is not a learning disability or sheer stupidity. The Hebrew root means "open" and suggests the imagery of an open door. Many Hebrew words paint vivid images. As a rule, Hebrew is not abstract, esoteric, or theoretical like Greek. This particular expression is a classic example. It embodies the Hebrew idea of what it means to be simple minded: a door left standing open.

People today like to be thought of as open minded. To an Old Testament Jew, that would be the essence of half-wittedness. To say that you had an open mind would be to declare your ignorance. It would be very much like modern agnosticism. Agnostics pretend to have an enlightened worldview, and the typical agnostic likes to assume the air and attitudes of an intellectual who is privy to advanced understanding. But the word *agnostic* itself is a combination of two Greek words meaning "without knowledge." It is a declaration of one's ignorance. The Latin equivalent would be *ignoramus*.

It's neither healthy nor praiseworthy to have a constantly open mind with regard to one's beliefs, values, and moral convictions. An open door permits everything to go in and out. It is the very attitude that makes so many people today vacillating, indecisive, double minded—unstable in all their ways (Jas. 1:8). They have no anchor for their thoughts, no rule by which to distinguish right from wrong, and therefore no real convictions. They simply lack the tools and mental acuity to discern or make careful distinctions. That way of thinking is nothing to be proud of.

Tell a devout Old Testament believer that you are open minded and he might say, "Well, close the door." You need to know what to keep in and what to keep out. You have a door on your house for that very reason. You close it to keep some things in (children, heat, air conditioning, or the family pet) and you want it to remain closed in order to keep some things out (burglars, insects, and door-to-door salesmen). You open it only when you *want* to let something or someone in. The door is a point of discretion. It's the place where you distinguish between what should be let in and what should be kept out. In fact, you probably have a hole with a lens in it that you can look through to help you in discerning who's going to get in and who's not.

Our minds should function in a similar fashion. There's no honor in letting things in and out indiscriminately. Close the door, and carefully guard what goes in and out (Prov. 4:23).

The Word of God has the effect of making simple minds wise for that very purpose. It teaches us discernment. It trains our senses "to discern good and evil" (Heb. 5:14).

The Hebrew word translated "wise" in Psalm 19:7 is not speaking of theoretical knowledge, philosophical sophistication, intellectual prowess, smooth speech, cleverness, or any of the other things that define worldly wisdom. Biblical wisdom is about prudent living. The word *wise* describes someone who walks and acts sensibly and virtuously: "He who trusts in his own heart is a fool, but he who walks wisely will be delivered" (Prov. 28:26). The truly wise person recognizes what is good and right, then applies that simple truth to everyday life.

In other words, the wisdom in view here has nothing to do with intelligence quotients or academic degrees. It has everything to do with truth, honor, virtue, and the fruit of the Spirit. Indeed, "the fear of the Lord is the beginning of wisdom, and the knowledge of the Holy One is understanding" (Prov. 9:10).

There's only one document in the entire world that can revive a spiritually dead soul and make him spiritually wise. No book penned by mere men could possibly do that, much less give us skill to live life well in a world cursed by sin. There is no spiritual life, salvation, or sanctification apart from Scripture.

We all desperately need that transformation. It is not a change we can make for ourselves. All the glory on display in creation is not enough to accomplish it. *Only* Scripture has the life-giving, life-changing power needed to revive a spiritually dead soul and make the simple wise.

GOD'S WORD IS RIGHT, CAUSING JOY

Verse 8 gives a third statement about the perfect sufficiency of Scripture: "The precepts of the Lord are right, rejoicing the heart." The Hebrew noun translated "precepts" ("statutes" in some versions) denotes principles for instruction. Close English synonyms would be *canons, tenets, axioms, principles,* and even *commands*. All those shades of meaning are inherent in the word. It includes the principles that govern our character and conduct, as well as the propositions that shape our convictions and our confession of faith. It covers every biblical precept, from the basic ordinances governing righteous behavior to the fundamental axioms of sound doctrine. All of these are truths to be believed.

That's because they are "right"—not merely right as opposed to wrong (although that's obviously true). The Hebrew word means "straight" or "undeviating." It has the connotation of uprightness, alignment, and perfect order. The implication is that the precepts of Scripture keep a person going the right direction, true to the target.

Notice that there is progress and motion in the language. The effect of God's Word is not static. It regenerates, restoring the soul to life. It enlightens, taking a person who lacks discretion and transforming him into one who is skilled in all manner of living. It then sanctifies—setting us on a right path and pointing us in a truer direction. "Your word is a lamp to my feet and a light to my path" (Ps. 119:105).

But Scripture is not only a lamp and a light; it is the living voice that tells us, "This is the way, walk in it" when we veer to the right or the left (Isa. 30:21). We desperately need that guidance. "There is a way which seems right to a man, but its end is the way of death" (Prov. 16:25). Scripture makes the true way straight and clear for us.

The result is joy: "The precepts of the Lord are right, rejoicing the heart" (Ps. 19:8). If you are anxious, fearful, doubting, melancholy, or otherwise troubled in heart, learn and embrace God's precepts. The truth of God's Word will not only inform and sanctify you; it will also bring joy and encouragement to your heart.

This is true *especially* in times of trouble. Worldly wisdom's typical answers to despondency and depression are all empty, useless, or worse. Every form of self-help, self-esteem, and self-indulgence promises joy, but in the end such things just bring more despair. The truth of Scripture is a sure and time-tested anchor for troubled hearts. And the joy it brings is true and lasting.

The life-giving, life-changing power mentioned in verse 7 is the reason for the joy mentioned in verse 8. David knew that joy firsthand. So did the author of Psalm 119, who wrote, "This is my comfort in my affliction, that Your word has revived me" (Ps. 119:50). "I have remembered Your ordinances from of old, O Lord, and comfort myself" (v. 52). "Your statutes are my songs in the house of my pilgrimage" (v. 54). Clearly this is a major theme in Psalm 119: "I shall delight in Your commandments, which I love" (v. 47).

Jeremiah is sometimes called "the weeping prophet" because so much of his message is full of sorrow and grieving. Most scholars believe he is also the prophet who wrote the biblical book of Lamentations. No one listened to Jeremiah. Finally, they threw him in a pit to shut him up. But the prophet drew profound joy from the Word of God: "Your words became for me a joy and the delight of my heart; for I have been called by Your name, O Lord

God of hosts" (Jer. 15:16).

Christians are admonished to cultivate the joy that God's Word produces: "Let the word of Christ richly dwell within you, with all wisdom teaching and admonishing one another with psalms and hymns and spiritual songs, singing with thankfulness in your hearts to God" (Col. 3:16). The joyful heart depicted in verses like that is one of the key reasons Scripture is given to believers. As the apostle John greeted the recipients of his first inspired epistle, he said, "These things we write, so that our joy may be made complete" (1 John 1:4). On the night before His crucifixion, when Jesus's final instructions to His disciples were nearly complete, He told them, "These things I have spoken to you so that My joy may be in you, and that your joy may be made full" (John 15:11).

GOD'S WORD IS PURE, ENLIGHTENING THE EYES

Psalm 19:8 continues, "The commandment of the Lord is pure, enlightening the eyes." This speaks of Scripture as a book of commands. The expression underscores the Bible's inherent authority. It is not a book of recommendations or suggestions. It is not a collection of thought-provoking proposals or helpful-but-optional advice. Its precepts are binding commandments from the sovereign King of the universe, whose authority extends to every minuscule detail of our lives.

Even the call to believe the gospel is a command. "This is His commandment, that we believe in the name of His Son Jesus Christ, and love one another, just as He commanded us" (1 John 3:23). The summons to repentance likewise comes as a command: "God is now declaring to men that all people everywhere should repent" (Acts 17:30). The instructions given to us in Scripture are mandatory, because the Bible is the Word of God. Belief in, and obedience to, the Scriptures is not optional. So David simply refers to all of Scripture as "the commandment of the Lord."

And the commandment of the Lord is "pure." The Hebrew word means "clear." The Word of God is transparent; it is translucent; it is not murky or opaque. This is an affirmation of Scripture's *perspicuity*. In other words, the essential truth of the Bible is easily understood. God's Word expresses its meaning with sufficient clarity. Indeed, "Some things [are] hard to understand, which the untaught and unstable distort, as they do also the rest of the Scriptures, to their own destruction" (2 Pet. 3:16). But the fundamental truths of Scripture are clear enough that "those who walk on the way; even if they are fools, they shall not go astray" (Isa. 35:8, ESV). You do not need to have advanced intelligence or superhuman skill to understand the basic truth of the Bible. As a rule, Scripture is simply not very hard to understand. Again, the author of Psalm 119 echoes and expands on this theme: "The unfolding of Your words gives light; it gives understanding to the simple" (v. 130).

Far from being inherently mysterious or cryptic, Scripture is divine *revelation*. It is an unveiling of truth that would be impossible to understand if God Himself did not disclose it to us. It "is pure [clear, lucid], enlightening the eyes" (Ps. 19:8). The Bible shines light into our darkness, gives knowledge that overthrows our ignorance, and brings understanding to clear away our confusion. This is how the apostle Paul said it in 2 Corinthians 3:16: "Whenever a person turns to the Lord, the veil is taken away." Indeed, "'things which eye has not seen and ear has not heard, and which have not entered the heart of man, all that God has prepared for those who love Him.' For to us God revealed them through the Spirit; for the Spirit searches all things, even the depths of God" (1 Cor. 2:9–10).

Of course, only genuine believers benefit from the enlightening effect of God's Word. Paul goes on to say, "A natural man does not accept the things of the Spirit of God, for they are foolishness to him; and he cannot understand them, because they are spiritually appraised" (v. 14). In the words of Jesus, God has deliberately "hidden these things from the wise and intelligent and has revealed them to infants" (Matt. 11:25). Therefore, those who are wise in their own eyes gain little or nothing from the light of God's Word, while those with childlike faith receive it gladly and are thereby made *truly* wise. Jesus said, "Truly I say to you, whoever does not receive the kingdom of God like a child will not enter it at all" (Mark 10:15). The truth of Scripture is not some esoteric secret that a Gnostic guru must unlock for us. The faith required to accept it is simple, childlike trust.

Jesus taught and stressed those things against the backdrop of a very complex, confusing, allegorical, mystical interpretation of the Old Testament that was perpetuated by many of the rabbis of His time. "And the common people heard Him gladly" (Mark 12:37, NKJV).

God's commandments are clear. If they were not, they would be pointless. How could God hold us responsible to obey what we couldn't possibly understand? Therefore, to say the Bible isn't clear is to accuse God of deliberately confounding humanity. Scripture *is* clear—enlightening the eyes. Mark Twain was a hardened agnostic, and he is often quoted as saying, "It's not the things I don't understand in the Bible that bother me. It's the things I *do* understand."

That says it well. The problem for unbelievers is not that the Bible isn't clear enough. It's that God's Word is *absolutely* clear about the human problem—sin—and fallen people simply don't like what the Bible says. So in order to escape what is plain and easily apparent, they sometimes claim it's murky and indistinct. Believers know otherwise.

GOD'S WORD IS CLEAN, ENDURING FOREVER

Psalm 19:9 adds a fifth facet: "The fear of the Lord is clean, enduring forever." "The fear of the Lord" is a reference to the passion evoked in believers when their minds are awakened to the truth of Scripture. The subject hasn't changed. The poetic parallelism makes it clear that David is still talking about the Bible, and in this statement he is referring to the sense of righteous trepidation a sinful soul feels before God when the Word of God awakens the heart and mind. This is not the craven fear of contempt and revulsion; it is the reverential awe that is the basis for true worship.

The Bible is a perfect handbook on worship. It reveals the majesty and perfection of YHWH, the God of Abraham, Isaac, and Jacob (Ex. 3:6; Matt. 22:32)—the One who is the God and Father of our Lord Jesus Christ (Rom. 15:6). He is the Creator, Sustainer, and Sovereign of the universe. He alone is holy, omniscient, omnipresent, omnipotent, immutable, and eternal.

Scripture tells us not only *who* is to be worshiped, but also *how* He is to be worshiped. He is a Spirit, and He is to be worshiped in Spirit and in truth (John 4:23–24)—not through graven images, as if He were an idol or some manmade thing. Jesus said, "The Father is seeking . . . people to worship him" (v. 23, ESV).

As a manifesto and manual on worship, Scripture is "clean, enduring forever" (Psa. 19:9). The Hebrew word translated "clean" is the same word used more than ninety times in the Old Testament to speak of ceremonial cleanness. It means there is no impurity, defilement, or imperfection of any kind in Scripture. God's Word is without corruption; hence, it is without error.

Elsewhere, David makes that point even more emphatically, "The words of the Lord are pure words; as silver tried in a furnace on the earth, refined seven times" (Ps. 12:6). Notice that the very words of Scripture are totally free from all imperfections. There is no dross, no blemish, no foreign element. It would be hard to devise a more emphatic statement of biblical inerrancy.

And the proof of this absolute perfection is that the Word of God endures forever. It never changes. Any alteration to the text could only introduce imperfection. Scripture is eternally, unalterably perfect. Jesus said, "Heaven and earth will pass away, but My words will not pass away" (Matt. 24:35; Mark 13:31). "Truly I say to you, until heaven and earth pass away, not the smallest letter or stroke shall pass from the Law until all is accomplished" (Matt. 5:18). Scripture is full of similar statements: "Forever, O Lord, Your word is settled in heaven" (Ps. 119:89). "The grass withers, the flower fades, but the word of our God stands forever" (Isa. 40:8).

"'The word of the Lord endures forever.' And this is the word which was preached to you" (1 Pet. 1:25).

GOD'S WORD IS TRUE, ALTOGETHER RIGHTEOUS

The closing phrase of Psalm 19:9 gives us the last of these six poetic statements about God's Word: "The judgments of the Lord are true; they are righteous altogether." "Judgments" is from a Hebrew word that means "verdict." It is courtroom terminology, and it can refer to a decision, an ordinance, a legal right, a statutory privilege, a judicial sentence, or a decree. The word envisions God as the Judge, Lawgiver, and the One who grants all rights and privileges. All His judgments are true, and all His decrees are right.

And as the context makes clear, David still specifically has in mind the content of Scripture. All the Bible's statements are true, and its moral principles are "righteous altogether."

Scripture is the divine Magistrate's verdict on everything that pertains to life and godliness. When Scripture speaks, it is conclusive because it is God's own verdict. It is an immutable decree from the judgment seat of heaven. And "shall not the Judge of all the earth deal justly?" (Gen. 18:25). God's judgments are by definition *true*.

This is a crucial statement, and it establishes the starting point and the foundation for a truly Christian worldview. In a world of lies and deception, Scripture alone is absolutely, unequivocally "true" and "righteous altogether." There is no room in that expression for any view of Scripture that allows for historical blunders, scientific errors, factual inaccuracies, or fallacies of any kind. David could not have made a more thorough or definitive statement about the inerrancy and sufficiency of Scripture. The same point is echoed in Psalm 119:160: "The sum of Your word is truth, and every one of Your righteous ordinances is everlasting." Scripture is true in its entirety; and it is likewise true in the smallest particulars. To speak more precisely, it is *truth*. This is what Scripture consistently claims for itself. It is Jesus's own view of the Scriptures. He prayed,

"Sanctify [My disciples] in the truth; Your word is truth" (John 17:17).

Of course, most of the world rejects the Bible. It's not that the Bible is unbelievable—untold millions across the span of human history have believed Scripture, and their hearts and lives have been transformed by it. The reason obstinate unbelief is so widespread is that people simply don't *want* to believe Scripture, because it gives such a devastating analysis of the human condition, and it condemns those who love their sin. To unbelievers in Jesus's audience, He said,

> Why do you not understand what I am saying? It is because you cannot hear My word. You are of your father the devil, and you want to do the desires of your father. He was a murderer from the beginning, and does not stand in the truth because there is no truth in him. Whenever he speaks a lie, he speaks from his own nature, for he is a liar and the father of lies. But because I speak the truth, you do not believe Me. . . . He who is of God hears the words of God; for this reason you do not hear them, because you are not of God. (John 8:43–47)

But don't miss the central point of Psalm 19. Scripture is not only true, inerrant, and authoritative; it is also *sufficient.* It gives us every truth that really matters. It shows us the way of salvation and then equips us for every good work (2 Tim. 3:15–17). It is "righteous altogether"—actually fostering righteousness in those who accept it.

Scripture is eternally true, always applicable, and perfectly sufficient to meet all our spiritual needs. Contrary to what many people today think, the Bible does not need to be supplemented with new revelations. It does not need to be reinterpreted to accommodate the latest scientific theories. It does not need to be corrected to harmonize with whatever psychotherapy is currently popular. It certainly does not need to be edited to make it conform to postmodern notions about morality and relativism. All those things will come and go. "But the word of the Lord endures forever"

(1 Pet. 1:25)—as unchanged and unchanging as the God who gave it to us.

No.5

NOT ASHAMED OF THE GOSPEL

BY DR. MARTYN LLOYD-JONES

> For I am not ashamed of the gospel of Christ: for it is the power of God unto salvation to every one that believeth; to the Jew first, and also to the Greek. For therein is the righteousness of God revealed from faith to faith: as it is written, "The just shall live by faith." (Rom. 1:16–17)[1]

We start here a new section of the chapter because, at the end of verse 15, in a sense, the apostle has come to the end of his personal references to himself and his calling. In the first six and a half verses he has been making a general statement about his calling as an apostle. Then from there until the end of verse 15 he has been speaking of himself and his relationship to these particular Christians at Rome. Now, having dealt with that, he moves on, and

[1] Unless otherwise noted, Scripture quotations in this chapter are from the King James Version.

here he comes to make an announcement of the great theme of the epistle. It is, therefore, an important point of transition, and it is interesting to notice the way in which the apostle makes the transition. As someone has put it, he "glides" from one theme to another. There is no flourish about it. It is, in a sense, something very natural. He has hardly finished his previous theme before he starts the next with the word "For." In other words, he would have us see very clearly that it is a continuation of what he has been saying, and yet he is going to say something quite new.

Let us, then, remind ourselves of the context. "I am debtor," he says, "both to the Greeks, and to the Barbarians; both to the wise, and to the unwise. So, as much as in me is, I am ready to preach the gospel to you that are at Rome also. For I am not ashamed of the gospel of Christ: for it is the power of God unto salvation to every one that believeth; to the Jew first, and also to the Greek." In other words, he is saying that as he was ready to preach the gospel to Greeks and barbarians, wise and unwise, in the same way exactly he is ready to preach it in Rome. And he goes on to say why he is ready to preach it in Rome. And, of course, in doing so he incidentally tells them, tells us through them, tells all Christians everywhere, what is, after all, the great theme with which he constantly dealt. Had he been able to be there in person he would have preached to them on this theme, but since he cannot go to them personally, he will write to them. He will give them headings. In these two wonderful verses, therefore,—verses 16 and 17—he gives us, as it were, stated in a summary manner in the most succinct form conceivable, what is undoubtedly the great theme of apostolic preaching—the great theme, in particular, of this epistle to the Romans.

There is a difference between verse 16 and 17, and in this way; in verse 16 the apostle states his theme; in verse 17 he gives a general exposition of it. And you notice again the repetition of this word "for." "I am not ashamed of the gospel of Christ: *for* it is the power of God unto salvation to every one that believeth; to the Jew first, and also to the Greek: *for* therein a righteousness of God is revealed from faith to faith." And even later we shall find, in verse

18, "*for* the wrath of God is revealed . . ." (emphases added).

Now it is interesting, here, to observe Paul's style and method; you notice how logical he is, how he reasons from step to step. He is not one of those men who throw out anyhow, somehow, brilliant thoughts. No, his essential method is this reasoning method. We have noticed, and had occasion to emphasize already, that sometimes he is so moved and carried away by what he is talking about, that he even forgets to keep his thoughts orderly, but his mind was essentially a logical one, a clear-thinking and a reasoning one. It is the tremendous power of the truth that occasionally overwhelms him and makes him begin to sing or to indulge in some mighty apostrophe to God; but normally, I say, order and logic are his great characteristics. He "reasoned" from the Scriptures, we are told in the book of Acts; he "alleged," he "proved," he "demonstrated." That was the apostle's essential method. So here, then, he announces the theme in verse 16, gives a general exposition in verse 17, and in verse 18 he begins to work it out in detail.

It is obvious, then, I think, that we are at a very important and momentous point in our study of this great epistle. I suppose that, in a sense, there are no two verses of greater importance in the whole of Scripture than the two verses which we are now considering. You remember that these verses were in a sense responsible for the Protestant Reformation—from the standpoint of Protestantism and evangelicalism they are crucial, vital verses. We must never forget that. It was the realization that came to him of what exactly was being said to him through these two verses that proved to be the turning point in the life of Martin Luther. And it has subsequently been the turning point for many another, sometimes through Luther and his works, sometimes quite independently of Luther, but a similar thing has happened. Here, then, is the very rock bottom and foundation of Protestantism as over against Catholicism—Roman Catholicism in particular, but in reality all forms of Catholicism, every type of teaching that exalts the sacraments, and so on—here is the basis of all opposition to that kind of teaching. And, of course, it is the basis also of opposition to all attempts on the part of men to justify themselves by their own works and deeds and efforts in the sight of God. These two verses, therefore, are of crucial importance in the matter of evangelism also, because unless we are perfectly clear as to what they teach, somewhere or another we shall go wrong in our evangelism, either in our message or in our methods.

Let us look, then, at the great statement which is made here in these two verses. The first thing we notice as we examine verse 16 is the extraordinary way in which the apostle introduces his statement: "So, as much as in me is, I am ready to preach the gospel to you that are at Rome also, for I am not ashamed of the gospel of Christ." Now why did he put it like that? Well, let us start right at the beginning. The kind of expression, the figure of speech, which he uses here—"I am not ashamed of . . ." is known as litotes—and litotes means "an assertion which is made in the form of the negative of a contrary assertion." Instead of saying here that he is "proud" of the gospel, the apostle says that he is "not ashamed" of it. And to say that he is not ashamed of the gospel is another way of saying that he really glories in it, and that he boasts of it. He says, in writing to the Galatians, "God forbid that I should glory save in the cross of the Lord Jesus Christ" (6:14). He did glory in it. He gloried in the preaching of the cross. But here he chooses to put it like this—"I am not ashamed of it."

He did the same thing exactly, you remember, on another famous occasion when he was in trouble from a mob in Jerusalem. The captain of the Roman legion stationed in the city sent down his troops to deliver and to save him, so Paul began to have a conversation with him, and claimed to be "a citizen of no mean city" (Acts 21:39)—referring to Tarsus. Instead of saying that he was the citizen of a very important city, he put it in that other way. Now that is the way in which he speaks here; he really is telling these Romans that he is very ready, indeed, to preach the gospel at Rome; he is ready to preach it anywhere, and without apology, so he puts his assertion in this particular form.

Why, we may ask, did he choose to put this in that semi-negative manner? Well, as I understand it, this is something which he does quite deliberately. I think he does it partly not only to make a statement about himself, but also to help the people who were members of the church at Rome. There were people who, though they were Christians, were somewhat ashamed of the gospel. It seems to me to be abundantly clear that even a man like Timothy was a little guilty of that. "Be not thou therefore ashamed of the testimony of our Lord," writes Paul to him, "nor of me his prisoner" (2 Tim. 1:8). And the greatest thing he can say, later, about Onesiphorus—and it is tremendous praise—is that when Paul was in Rome, "he sought me out very diligently, and found me," and "he oft refreshed me and was not ashamed of my chain" (2 Tim. 1:16). Many people were ashamed. They knew that Paul was there, but they pretended they did not know it. They did not want to be associated with him; they were ashamed of the gospel. And undoubtedly there were people who were somewhat given to that in Rome itself.

So the apostle, I take it, puts it in this particular manner in order to help them, and in order to strengthen and also to deliver them out of this spirit of fear. Take the great word that he used in 2 Timothy 1:7, "For God hath not given us the spirit of fear; but of power, and of love, and of a sound mind"—that is, of discipline. So Paul is telling Timothy to rouse himself, to stir up the gift that is in him and which was given by the laying on of the hands of the presbytery. Rake the fire, says the apostle. Don't let it smoulder. Rake it a bit, liven it up, brighten it, make it burst into flame again. I take it, then, that he was doing something similar here with these Roman Christians. Indeed, it may be right to go even further than that, and I am not disposed to disagree with those who say that Paul himself had known what it was at times to be tempted along that line of being ashamed of the gospel. I am not saying that he ever was; I am saying that the devil may have tempted him along that line, as he has tempted many another a servant of God since then. So the apostle may be using this particular form of speech in order to show how he himself overcame that particular temptation.

But why should anybody ever be ashamed of the gospel? Do you know anything about this, my friends? It seems to me to be a very important question. And I am very ready to assert that if you have never known this particular temptation then it is probably due to the fact, not that you are an exceptionally good Christian, but that your understanding of the Christian message has never been clear. Let me substantiate that. It is never an impressive thing to hear a Christian saying, "Ever since I believed, I have never been tempted to doubt; I have never been tempted to shame." It is not good to say that. Whether it was actually true in the case of the apostle Paul or not, it was certainly true of Timothy. And if you read the lives of the saints, you will find that throughout the centuries, they have been attacked grievously along this particular line.

How does this arise? Well, let us look at some of the reasons. What tends to make a Christian sometimes ashamed of the gospel is the fact that the world always ridicules it, and regards it as utter folly. That was very true in the early days of the church. Paul, in writing to the Corinthians, says quite plainly that this gospel was "unto the Jews a stumblingblock, and unto the Greeks foolishness" (1 Cor. 1:23). They abominated the whole thing. The Pharisees hated it in the Lord Himself, and the Jews hated it always in the apostles. These Greeks, too, hated it in the same way. The world always ridicules the gospel, and man by nature does not like being ridiculed. He does not like to be associated with anything that is subject to ridicule.

Why, then, is it that the world ridicules the gospel? It is because of the message which the gospel conveys. The gospel proclaims—the preacher of the gospel has to proclaim—One who was born in utter, abject poverty. Born in a stable, no room at the inn! Brought up in a little village, trained as a carpenter! That is the One whom we preach. That is the One whom we hold before the world, One who was crucified in apparent weakness! Having made exalted claims for Himself, He is taken in utter helplessness. He is nailed to a tree, and dies while the mob jeers at Him and derides Him, saying, "He saved others; let him save himself, if he be the Christ, the chosen of God" (Luke 23:35). That is what we proclaim. We proclaim a carpenter, One who lived a life of poverty, and who died upon a cross. And, of course, the world scoffs at it and ridicules it in its heart, because we assert that this selfsame person is the Saviour of the world, and the Son of God. To the Jews it was a stumblingblock, and to the Greeks foolishness. So the very character of the message tends to produce this ridicule, and, as I say, man by nature does not like being ridiculed, so he is ashamed of this gospel. That is the temptation.

To put it in another way, the gospel is not a philosophy; it is a statement of a number of facts. Now the world never ridicules philosophy; it likes it. It is very learned and wonderful. You put up the rival views, and you discuss them in a condescending manner. The world likes that. But the gospel is not philosophy. There is no great philosophical argument here. Four gospels with an account of this person; then the account of His death; then the extraordinary claims that were made by very ignorant and simple people about Him, and the statements made—as they are made—in the book of Acts. It is not a philosophy. It does not follow the methods of philosophy. It is not a system of philosophy. And there, again, is something that tends to make the world ridicule it. And the apostle knew that full well. You remember how it happened, for instance—it is a perfect illustration of the whole thing—when Paul first visited Athens and began to speak there. The Stoics and Epicureans said, Who is this man? "What will this babbler say? He seemeth to be a setter forth of strange gods" (Acts 17:18). And when Paul began to preach to them, at once they began to ridicule, especially when he began to talk about the Lord Jesus Christ and His death and His resurrection. And the meeting broke up. This is not philosophy at all, they said; this man is just talking about some person. This is folly. This is nonsense. In other words, Paul was not a propounder of some new philosophical theory.

These, then, are the things that from time to time have made those who are truly Christian feel a certain amount of shame, especially when they are talking about these things in the presence of so-called learned and cultured, philosophically-minded people. And then, add to all that, of course, that the apostle was here writing to Christians in Rome—the mistress of the world, the imperial city, the seat of government, where all the great people always came. Just think of it. In the midst of the pomp and the ceremonial of those Roman emperors and the Roman court, there comes a man who says that the Saviour of the world was a carpenter from Nazareth, and Paul imagines the ridicule and the laughter of the court and the great people. The latest joke—a man has arrived who actually says that a carpenter from Nazareth in the land of the Jews is the Son of God and the Saviour of the world, and that He saves the world by dying helplessly upon a cross! How funny! How amusing! That is the response of the learned circles.

Now the apostle Paul was a man of mighty intellect. He was an able man, and it is neither an easy nor a simple thing for a man like that, endowed as he was, to endure this ridicule, this sarcasm, this scorn, and this derision. You will find his main exposition of these matters in the first three chapters of his first epistle to the Corinthians, and there is no doubt at all but that he felt the thing acutely. Here he was, with all his training, his background, and his ability, just preaching—in a way that anybody could preach as far as the matter was concerned—and as he spoke he was aware of what his hearers were saying, and he saw them looking at one another as he addressed them. So he says quite deliberately that he has become a fool for Christ's sake, and he goes on to say, 'If any man would be wise in this world, let him become a fool, that he may be wise." In other words, he says, You are interested in wisdom and you regard us as fools, but I tell you, if you want to be really wise you had better become fools with us, and then you will have God's wisdom.

But the play on this word "fool" indicates quite clearly that the apostle obviously had had to battle with this particular matter. The fact is that the world attaches great significance to mind, and to intellect, and to learning and to understanding. And not only that, but to moral effort and moral striving too. It glories in these things.

But the gospel does not. That does not mean that the gospel tells you to commit intellectual suicide, or that an able man cannot be a Christian. But it does mean that the gospel tells all men at the very beginning that it does not matter how able a man may be; that alone will never make him a Christian. It puts the able man on exactly the same level as those who are most lacking in intellect. It reduces all, as we have already seen, to a common level. It deliberately says that intellectual pride is probably the last citadel to give way when the Holy Spirit is dealing with a man's soul. The gospel does not glory in intellect. It does not glory in moral effort and striving. It tells you at the very beginning that you can do all you like and it will avail you nothing; that all your righteousnesses will be as "filthy rags," that all your wonderful works will be "dung" and "refuse"—of no use at all to you! Now the world hates that, and the apostle knew it. He had to suffer much from its sarcasm and its scorn, and therein came the temptation to be ashamed of the gospel, knowing what he did about the mentality of the Greeks and the Jews, and of others who listen to this gospel. You see how easily the temptation could come in, and it came like that to Timothy. And then, when you add that they had even to suffer for this gospel, not only to suffer the ridicule, but to suffer physically, and so on, you can see well how this temptation would arise.

In other words, the gospel of Jesus Christ reverses the world's ideas in all respects and always, without exception. It is not in line with any other teaching. It is not in line with any other philosophy. It is absolutely on its own, and it is entirely different. The world is not intrigued and interested; it delights in great intellectual exercise. And here we stand and we say that the most untutored, the most illiterate person in the world tonight, can listen to the same gospel as the greatest philosopher, and by grace receive salvation. The world sits back and roars with laughter. Ah yes! but because a man is not yet perfect he does not like being laughed at, especially when he can talk philosophy to the man who is laughing at him. He knows that he could meet him on his own ground if he wanted to, but knows he must not do so, for thereby he would be denying his own gospel. He has to keep all that back and indeed to leave it out. He has to be a fool for Christ's sake. You see where the temptation comes in?

These considerations, it seems to me, constitute a most important test as to what is really the true gospel. You can really test what is being preached by one particular criterion, and it is this: The gospel of Jesus Christ is always offensive to the natural man. The gospel of Jesus Christ is always exposed to this charge of ridicule and contempt. And because of this, one of the best ways of testing the preaching or exposition of the gospel is just that: Is it offensive to the natural man? Will it annoy the natural man? Will the natural man hate it? I assert that if it does not do that, there is something wrong with it somewhere. The gospel of Jesus Christ is not popular with the natural man. He is against it. So that if you find the natural, unregenerate man praising either the preacher of his message then, I say, you had better examine that preaching and that preacher very carefully. Now we have all seen that there are many ways in which the gospel is presented which are not offensive. Have we not read or heard sermons from those who depict Christ as a great hero and example? Nobody has ever been offended by that; in fact the world likes it, and for this reason. You present Christ as a great exemplar, a great hero, and people will say, "That is fine, that is marvelous." What they are really saying is this: "Now I am going to follow Him; I am going to be like that. I can, of course! I have simply got to make the effort. If I do make the effort, I can do it." So they like it, they take it as a compliment. There He is, rise up and go after Him. And the people are ready to do it because they think they are capable of doing it. When you tell them that He is One whom they cannot imitate, that He condemns all, then they will begin to show their teeth and hate you for it; but present Him as a hero, as an example, it will not annoy them.

Or again, take Christ's teaching. The teaching of the Lord Jesus Christ is presented by some people as the most beautiful teaching in the world. The Sermon on the Mount, they say, is marvelous; it is beautiful and exalted. That is how they present it. The world likes it again for the same reason: It believes that it can take it up and put it into practice. But when the Sermon on the Mount is truly preached, when a man begins to know what it is to be "poor in spirit" and to "mourn," and to have a "hunger and thirst after righteousness," when he faces the real spiritual exposition of the law, he hates it because it condemns him; he does not want to feel "poor in spirit" (Matt. 5:3–4, 6). As a man, whose sermon I once read, put it: "These hymns by Charles Wesley, which make you say 'Vile and full of sin I am,' ought to be expunged from the hymn book. Who ever heard of a man applying for a job, going to an employer and saying, 'I am vile and full of sin'—if he did he would never get a job, and, fancy, we are told to say that." He hated it because it condemned him. Yes, but if we preach the gospel as a beautiful teaching it will never annoy; it will never hurt.

Or, in the same way, how often is the Lord Jesus Christ presented as someone who can help us with our problems? You know the type of preaching. "Are you in trouble? Is some particular sin getting you down? Is something worrying you? Come to Christ; He will put you right. Come at once. He is waiting for you, and He will take all your troubles away, and you will walk with a light step tomorrow—you won't know yourself. All your problems will have gone. Come to Him." That never offends anybody; how could it? Such a "gospel" cannot offend people, because they are in trouble and they want help, and here is someone who is ready to help them at any moment. They only have to come to Him and He will do everything for them. Oh, how often has the Christ, the Son of God, been preached as if He were but a super-psychologist, who can help people to resolve their difficulties and to solve their problems and put everything right, and make them happy once and for ever! That does not offend anybody. Or if His teaching and He Himself are presented as some kind of noble, ethical moral uplift, giving a wonderful philosophy of life—the pale Galilean, the aesthetic poet, the delicate one who is too refined for the world, which could not follow Him, and as they drove Socrates to drink hemlock, so they crucified Him, and so on—that never annoys anybody at all. It just puts Christ among the philosophers. He is one of them, and you admire them all together in the same way.

Oh, let me end this list by putting the matter like this: Do you know it is even possible to preach the cross of Christ in a way that makes people applaud it? They say, How beautiful! How wonderful! It is possible to preach it in such a way that it does not offend anybody. And yet, says the apostle, if I do certain things, then will the offence of the cross have ceased. When the cross is truly preached it is a stumblingblock to Jews, it is folly to the Greeks. They hate it. It is an offence. And it is an offence to the natural man today. But oftentimes the cross is preached as something pitiful, and Christ as a man to be pitied. Is it not so? "What a shame! Too bad! The world did not know Him. It did not recognize Him. In its cruelty it put Him to death. But He even forgave them there, and smiled upon them. Wonderful Jesus!!" That is not the preaching of the cross. There is no offence in that. That has never annoyed anybody at all, because there you are depicting Him as one who was too good for this world, and whom the world crucified. That is not the offence of the cross.

The offence of the cross is this—that I am so condemned and so lost and so hopeless that if He, Jesus Christ, had not died for me, I would never know God, and I could never be forgiven. And that hurts, that annoys; that tells me I am hopeless, that I am vile, that I am useless; and as a natural man I do not like it. So you see the importance of all this. The gospel itself is something that produces the reaction of offence in people. They hate it. They ridicule it. They pour their sarcasm and scorn upon it. And the apostle knew that. He had known what it was to be ridiculed in various places. "What will this babbler say? Who is this fellow?" And he knew very well that when he went to Rome he would be subjected to the same thing. He knew that the true gospel produces this ridicule and opposition. And yet, you notice, he tells them that in spite of all these difficulties, he is ready to preach it. Oh, my friends, let us be clear about this; let us make certain of it. My assertion is that the gospel of the New Testament, when truly preached, arouses antagonism. The world does not praise it; it does the exact opposite.

Read the lives of the men whom God has used most signally in the history of the church from the very beginning until today, and you will find that they have all had to put up with this ridicule. Think of the great George Whitefield, and of John and Charles Wesley when they were preaching here in London two hundred years ago—the ridicule to which they were subjected, the epithets that were hurled at them, the contempt and the scorn and the sarcasm! The mighty Whitefield—great man even in a natural sense, conceivably one of the greatest orators that the world has ever known—yet in "polite society" in London, because, unfortunately, he had weakness in one of the muscles of his eyes and had a squint, he was known in the circles of the great as "Dr. Squintum." They ridiculed him and his gospel.

It was the same with regard to John and Charles Wesley; even their own relatives were guilty of it. They said in effect, "Look here, why must you make fools of yourselves? Why cannot you preach as other people are preaching? You have just got a mob of ordinary, common, ignorant people following you wherever you go. You will get them there in Kennington; you will get them in Moorfields; you will get them in Tottenham Court Road. You will get them all over the country. But your preaching is the preaching that appeals only to such people." Even their own mother spoke to them like that. That was the charge that was brought against them, and of course it used to hurt a man like John Wesley—a Fellow of his College in Oxford, an erudite, able man,—yet he stood up to it as the apostle did, and said, "I am not ashamed. I will be yet more vile." That is how the temptation comes. This, I say, is a very important matter, and a very great test of the preaching of the gospel. If it does not expose us to this charge of contempt, if there is not something about it that tends to make us feel ashamed at times of what we are preaching, then we are not preaching the true gospel. But the great thing is that the apostle, in spite of all that, says here, I am not ashamed of the gospel; though I may be the laughing-stock of Rome, I am coming. "I am not ashamed of the gospel of Christ."

Then Paul goes on to tell us why he is not ashamed of it—let me at this point just introduce this matter to you. Here is another most vital test. Let me put it to you in the form of a question. If you tell me you are not ashamed of the gospel, I have the right to ask you why you are not ashamed of it? I wonder what reason you would give? The point I want to make now is this, that the only true answer to give to that question is the one the apostle gives. But how often do people give other answers, which again reveal a failure to understand the true character of the gospel! Nothing is more revealing than the reasons people give for not being ashamed of the gospel.

Let me give you an illustration. I once heard a man giving his testimony, and this is how he put it: he said, "I took my decision for Christ twenty years ago and I have never regretted it!" Now he was not ashamed of the gospel of Christ; he said so. But you notice his reason? "I took my decision for Christ twenty years ago and I have never regretted it." That was the only reason, the one he always gave. What he meant by that, of course, was that the gospel of Christ had made him a happy man, and had delivered him in certain respects. But the whole of his reason, you see, was a purely subjective one. That is not what the apostle gives us. Are we clear, I wonder, about this matter? Our reason for not being ashamed of the gospel must always be special to the gospel. It must always be unique, and that means, of necessity, that it must not simply end with us and what has happened to us. "I am not ashamed of the gospel of Christ." Why? Because "it is the power of God unto salvation . . . For therein is the righteousness of God revealed from faith to faith." That is unique, is it not?

If you just put the answer in a personal, subjective way, do you see at once to what you are exposing yourself? If you get up and say, "I have believed in Christ now for a certain length of time; I am not ashamed of it, I have never regretted it—and I will tell you why—I have been so much happier since I believed it; I sleep much better than I used to do, I do not quarrel as I used to, people tell me that I am brighter and happier; I don't do certain things now which

I used to do before; that is my reason why I am not ashamed of the gospel; it has done all that for me"—what response will you get?

Very well, I listen as an unbeliever, and I say, "That is very interesting! Tomorrow night I will go to the First Church of Christ Scientist, because I hear that people there are also able to give marvelous testimonies." So I go to the Christian Science Church and I listen there and I hear the same thing. "The best day that ever came into my life was the day when I was taken by a friend in my trouble to one of the Christian Science meetings. I was worried and troubled; everything got me down; my health was suffering. I had been to the doctors; nothing could put me right; but since I believed this and began to practise it I have been absolutely different. My friends say they can scarcely recognize me. I am walking with a lighter step; I am happy; nothing troubles me at all, even when I am taken ill, it is nothing." The same thing! And so I go the round of all the cults and I find that they say the same thing. I even go and listen to a lecture by a psychologist, and he says the same thing, and he can put his cases forward and they will give the same testimony.

You see, my friends, how important it is that we should be able to give the right reason. It is not enough that you get up and say, "I am not ashamed of the gospel of Christ." The question is, What is your reason? And, God willing, we will go on to consider the great answer which is given by this mighty man of God. "I am not ashamed of the Gospel of Christ," he says, because it is God's gospel, and because it is God's power—God's dynamic; because it is salvation in its full content, because it is the true and only way of salvation, a certain way, a revealed way. It is a righteousness from God Himself. And there, you see, the apostle has introduced great words of theology, the great words of Christian doctrine. That is Paul's reason for not being ashamed. And I do not hesitate to assert that it is the only true reason; it is the only reason that really glorifies God and the Lord Jesus Christ, because all other reasons can be counterfeited by the other things. The reason for not being ashamed, for not being ashamed of this gospel, must be unique, separate, distinct. God glorified! Christ glorified! Glorying in the Spirit! Something that no one can say, save he who has been called by God's grace, born again, and given a new nature, and an understanding of how God has done it all! God willing, we will go on to consider the reasons which the apostle gives positively for his not being ashamed. I think you will agree with me when I say, How we ought to thank God for the fact that Paul did use litotes! How grateful we should be to him for putting it in the semi-negative form—"I am not ashamed . . ." and may God enable us all to speak in the same way.

No.6

THE STANDARD OF SOUND WORDS:

A Mandate for the Pulpit

BY STEVEN J. LAWSON

Retain the standard of sound words which you have heard from me, in the faith and love which are in Christ Jesus. (2 Tim. 1:13)

Fifty years of distinguished ministry in one place is a rare milestone to achieve, certainly a cause for great celebration. Such was the case with Charles Hodge, the renowned professor of theology at Princeton Theological Seminary. The date was April 24, 1872, as over four hundred former students gathered at the seminary and marched in formal procession to the First Presbyterian Church to honor their distinguished teacher. In the church sat the faculty, directors, and trustees of both Princeton College and Princeton Seminary, along with delegates from other seminaries and colleges. Missionaries were present from as far away as India, Africa, and Ireland.

Speaker after speaker hailed Hodge as the leading theological mind of his day. When it came time for Hodge to address those assembled, every person spontaneously rose to their feet. He called this occasion the "apex of my life."[1] In his brief remarks, he uttered what has become the defining statement of his life: "I am not afraid to say that a new idea never originated in this Seminary."[2] By this stunning confession, Hodge meant that he, along with the faculty, had not changed or added to the pure truth of holy Scripture. They had not chased theological fads. They had not departed from orthodoxy. They had not forsaken the sound doctrine of their forefathers. Over these five decades, Hodge had been a faithful guardian of the truth.

PROCLAIMING THE OLD TRUTHS

The "Prince of Preachers," Charles Haddon Spurgeon, said much the same. When faced in his day with the Downgrade Controversy, he chose to stay the course by retaining "the faith that was once for all delivered to the saints" (Jude 3, ESV). He declared,

> It is no novelty, then, that I am preaching; no new doctrine. I love to proclaim these strong old doctrines, which are called by nickname Calvinism, but which are surely and verily the revealed truth of God as it is in Christ Jesus. By this truth I make a pilgrimage into the past, and as I go, I see father after father, confessor after confessor, and martyr after martyr, standing up to shake hands with me.[3]

By this assertion, this famed preacher testified that he continued to proclaim the old truths as they had been passed down to him. He

---

[1] Archibald Alexander Hodge, *The Life of Charles Hodge* (New York: Charles Scribner's Sons, 1880), 530.

[2] Ibid., 521.

[3] Charles Spurgeon, "Election," Sermons 41-42 in *The New Park Street Pulpit*, vol. 1 (London: Passmore & Alabaster, 1855), 313.

held fast the standard of sound words as it had been entrusted to him.

Spurgeon maintained,

> Theology hath nothing new in it except that which is false. The preaching of Paul must be the preaching of the minister to-day. There is no advancement here. We may advance in our knowledge of it; but it stands the same, for this good reason, that it is perfect, and perfection cannot be any better. The old truth that Calvin preached, that Chrysostom preached, that Paul preached, is the truth that I must preach to-day, or else be a liar to my conscience and my God. I can not shape the truth. I know of no such thing as paring off the rough edges of a doctrine. John Knox's gospel is my gospel. That which thundered through Scotland must thunder through England again. . . . For wherever there is not the old gospel we shall find "Ichabod" written upon the church walls ere long. The old truth of the Covenanters, the old truth of the Puritans, the old truth of the Apostles, is the only truth that will stand the test of time, and never need to be altered to suit a wicked and ungodly generation. Christ Jesus preaches to-day the same as when he preached upon the mount; he hath not changed his doctrines; men may ridicule and laugh, but still they stand the same—*semper idem* written upon every one of them. They shall not be removed or altered.[4]

Spurgeon rightly understood the necessity of this theological continuity from one generation to the next. Cultures change. Seasons change. Fashions change. But the truth never changes.

A STRICTER ACCOUNTABILITY

The truth of Scripture is a sacred trust that has been committed

[4] Charles Spurgeon, "The Immutability of Christ," Sermon 170 in *The New Park Street Pulpit*, vol. 4 (London: Passmore & Alabaster, 18[illegible]), 4[illegible] 45.

to every man of God sovereignly called to preach the Word. He is directly accountable to God for the truth recorded in the written Word of God that has been placed in his hands. *Every* preacher has been solemnly charged to retain the standard of sound words that has been entrusted to him. He is appointed a steward of the truth, and he must be faithful to persevere. In the end, he must answer to God for this stewardship. "Let not many of you become teachers, my brethren, knowing that as such we will incur a stricter judgment" (Jas. 3:1). Every preacher is responsible to God to preach the truth as it has been handed down to him in Scripture. A greater condemnation awaits the one who departs from this standard of truth.

It is not enough that the man of God begin his ministry grounded in the Word of God. When he comes to the end of his life, he must be found faithful to the saving message recorded in the Scripture. It does not suffice that he started his ministry well if he does not end his gospel labors well. It is not enough that he believed the message entrusted to him at the outset of his work. He must maintain his allegiance to the trust that has been placed into his hands. He must finish the course, having kept the faith.

LAST WORDS FROM PRISON

Understanding this critical nature of retaining sound doctrine, the apostle Paul issued a final charge to Timothy concerning its great importance. In this signature text, Paul commands, "Retain the standard of sound words which you have heard from me, in the faith and love which are in Christ Jesus" (2 Tim. 1:13). As the apostle writes these words, he has come to the end of his life. This itinerate preacher has been arrested by the Roman authorities and imprisoned for the second time in Rome. During his first Roman imprisonment, some five to seven years earlier, he was held under house arrest for two long years. During that time, Paul learned that his life would be spared and that he would be released. But this time would be different. This veteran preacher knew that his life would not be extended.

Confined in the Mamertine prison, Paul is suffering from exposure to the bitter cold in this damp hellhole. Only Luke is with him. In a short time, he will be taken out of this prison cell, and tradition tells us that he will be led to the outskirts of town, where his head will be severed on the Ostian Way. He will pay the ultimate price and die for the very truth that he has faithfully preached.

This second letter to Timothy is his final communication with the outside world. Last words should be lasting words. This is no time to address lesser matters of secondary importance. This is the opportune moment to speak what is primary, not what is peripheral. Paul now emphasizes what is of utmost consequence in ministry. Here is what is most essential to gospel labors. Timothy must retain the sacred stewardship of sound words that has been invested in him. The truth is absolutely fundamental in advancing God's work.

EVERY PREACHER'S MANDATE

Here is a mandate for every pulpit. This charge has been laid at the feet of every preacher whom God calls into gospel ministry. What is stated here is binding upon every preacher who would follow in Timothy's footsteps. Every man who stands before an open Bible today must be faithful to retain this same standard of sound words. Every servant of the truth must hold fast to sound doctrine as it is recorded in Scripture.

In this chapter, our focus is singularly upon what Paul writes in 2 Timothy 1:13. This is what Paul required of Timothy. Similarly, it is what God requires of each of His messengers in their time and place in history. Let us now consider seven truths stated in this important text.

THE CHARGE TO OBEY

First, Paul begins with a straightforward charge to Timothy,

"Retain the standard of sound words." This is no mere option for his young son in the faith to weigh. Nor is this to be regarded as a suggestion for him to consider. Instead, this charge comes to Timothy in the form of an apostolic command. This solemn charge is given "in the presence of God and of Christ Jesus, who is to judge the living and the dead, and by His appearing and His kingdom" (2 Tim. 4:1). No more sobering charge could be issued, as Paul invokes the first two persons of the Godhead to bear witness. This command demands Timothy's full compliance and unwavering allegiance. There is no middle ground in this matter. He cannot straddle the fence. Timothy will either obey or disobey this charge.

The essence of this charge is that Timothy must "retain" the sound words he has been taught by Paul. This word (Gk., *echo*) means "to hold on to, to have in the hand." The idea is maintaining a strong hold on something with a tight grip. This word denotes laying hold of something with a forceful grasp that will not let it go. For example, this same word was used of the sword that was securely fastened to Peter's side (John 18:10). This word indicates that Timothy must hold fast to the truth he heard from Paul. As his ministry continues, he is never to abandon the primary focus of this charge.

"Retain" is a verb that needs to be parsed in order to see its full richness. It is recorded in the present tense, meaning this "standard of sound words" must *always* be maintained. No matter what would threaten to cause him to loosen his grip on the truth, he must firmly retain it. Moreover, "retain" is in the active voice, indicating that Timothy must take action to adhere to the truth. He cannot sit back and be a passive observer in this matter. Further, "retain" is in the imperative mood. This means it is an apostolic command necessitating his full obedience. The full force of this charge cannot be overstated. It comes with an arresting authority upon Timothy's conscience. He must never release his hold upon the doctrines that Paul has deposited into his life. He must maintain his possession of these sound words and never surrender the deposit of truth that has been entrusted to him.

THE STANDARD TO KEEP

Second, Paul calls the stewardship entrusted to Timothy "the standard of sound words." This word "standard" (Gk., *hupotupōsis*) describes the outward form of something that serves as a reliable guide. The term was used to depict Paul's conversion as an "example" to all of God's mercy (1 Tim. 1:16). In the first century, this word described the initial rough sketch that was drawn by an artist. This drawing provided the well-defined parameters within which it must be completed. There could be no coloring outside the lines. As this relates to Timothy, he must stay within the clearly marked boundaries of sound doctrine. This same word was also used to describe the initial outline that an author would write as the structure for his book. This charted the flow of thought for the entire book. The manuscript must follow this set pattern that was established if it is to accomplish its original goal.

In this case, the "standard" that has been laid down for Timothy must be observed. Whatever Timothy will preach must meet this "standard." He may not depart from it and teach something else. This apostolic pattern will remain unchanging for Timothy, regardless of the culture in which he serves. It will be the same for him, no matter what church he will serve. Everything must be in alignment with this highest standard. It is "the norm of norms that cannot be normed." This unalterable standard for Timothy is biblical, not cultural. It is objective, not subjective; black and white, not shades of gray; divine, not human; heavenly, not earthly; timeless, not temporal.

THE WORDS TO RETAIN

Third, this divinely-set standard is comprised of individual "words" (Gk., *logos*). These are specific words that have come from God that have definite meanings. These words can be studied, parsed, and defined. This standard has not come in vague notions or indefinite, ambivalent ideas. They have not been given in broad, general thoughts that merely convey nebulous concepts. Rather, this standard has been recorded with distinct "words" that can be delineated and defended. They are definite words whose meaning must be preached, understood, believed, and lived.

The words are "sound" (Gk., *hugiaino*), which means "well being, healthy." When a person's body is physically well, we say he is in sound health. This Greek word was sometimes used in the four gospels to refer to people whom Jesus healed (Luke 7:10). They had suffered a disease or disability, but Jesus made them whole. As it relates to Timothy, he must retain the "sound," spiritually healthy words received from Paul. That is, they are free from the soul-threatening diseases of worldly philosophy or false teaching. These words are pure, free from any mixture of heretical error. Paul later used this word to refer to "sound doctrine" (2 Tim. 4:3; Titus 2:1). Sound words are healthy words that promote spiritual well-being.

Elsewhere in the book of 2 Timothy, Paul describes these "sound words" in many other terms. Throughout this letter, they are identified as "the gospel" (1:8), "the treasure" (1:14), "the rules" of the competition (2:5), "the word of God" (2:9), "the word of truth" (2:15), "the truth" (2:18; 2:25; 3:7, 8; 4:4), "the faith" (3:8; 4:7), "my teaching" (3:10), "the things you have learned" (3:14), "the sacred writings" (3:15), and as "Scripture" (3:16), "the word" (4:2), "sound doctrine" (4:3), and "our teaching" (4:15). Timothy must hold fast to these "sound words" for the entirety of his ministry.

THE PRESSURES TO RESIST

Fourth, this apostolic charge implies that there will be many sinister forces that will try to pry loose Timothy's grip upon the truth. Paul's young son in the faith will be confronted with countless forms of false teaching that are diametrically opposed to the biblical standard that was passed down by Paul. These foul heresies include various forms of legalism, syncretism, humanism, Gnosticism, Judaism, mysticism, asceticism, and many others.

These deadly teachings are contrary to the health-giving words that Paul entrusted to Timothy. These dangerous ideologies are poisonous, lethal, and destructive to the soul.

Timothy must resist all pressure to adopt any of these aberrant teachings. He must not allow anything to modify what Paul has taught him. In his first letter to Timothy, Paul had already warned him that "in later times some will fall away from the faith, paying attention to deceitful spirits and doctrines of demons" (1 Tim. 4:1). The apostle admonished him that there will always be a departure from the clear teaching found in Scripture. This falling away from the faith will occur even within the church itself—this is what makes it so deceptive. It is falsehood that is joined together with the truth. But half of a truth is no truth; a partial truth is, in reality, a lie.

Concerning this apostasy, Paul warned, "For the time will come when they will not endure sound doctrine; but wanting to have their ears tickled, they will accumulate for themselves teachers in accordance to their own desires, and will turn away their ears from the truth and will turn aside to myths" (2 Tim. 4:3–4). In the face of this frontal assault on the truth, Timothy must resist the lure to alter his message to meet the demands of carnal people. He must not yield the high ground that has been clearly articulated in these sound words. He must not allegorize away the purity of these truths, but retain the doctrine as it has been placed into his hands. He must hold fast to it exactly as he has received it from Paul.

THE CONTINUITY TO MAINTAIN

Fifth, Paul stressed to Timothy that there must be a seamless continuity in the transmission of these truths "which you have heard from me." In other words, Timothy must preach only what squares with what he has been taught by Paul. In a relay race, one runner must not only receive the baton from the other runner but also retain it. In like manner, Timothy must retain the truth exactly as he has received it from Paul. There must be an unrelenting hold on the truth by Timothy as he received it from his spiritual mentor.

There can be no exchanging of this standard for another system. There can be no modification of the gospel.

Paul further stressed the necessity of this uninterrupted continuity from one man to the next when he writes, "The things which you have heard from me in the presence of many witnesses, entrust these to faithful men who will be able to teach others also" (2 Tim. 2:2). There are four spiritual generations represented in this charge. The truth that Paul taught Timothy must be, in turn, passed down to "faithful men," who will then teach "others." There must be the ongoing transfer of the truth, from one man to the next, without any change in the message. What was taught in the first century by Paul to Timothy must be the same message that will be preached throughout the centuries. Timothy is a critical link in this living chain that must stretch in unbroken fashion from the apostles to their associates, to a long line of godly men, to the present.

A great price must be paid by Timothy as the truth is placed in his hands. Paul will tell Timothy, "All who desire to live godly in Christ Jesus will be persecuted" (2 Tim. 3:12). This doctrinal standard has been passed down to each successive generation on a sea of blood. Preachers have given their lives to uphold these sound words. God's messengers have been fed to the lions for their confession of these truths. They have been burned at the stake for remaining true to the faith. They have been put to death by the very ones to whom they preached the message. Every preacher bears this duty to be willing to suffer for the truth that they pass down to the next.

THE FAITH TO EXERCISE

Sixth, Paul reminds Timothy of the strong faith that he must have in Jesus Christ in order to fulfill this charge. At the end of the verse, the apostle asserted that Timothy must retain the truth "in the faith . . . which [is] in Christ Jesus." This means that Timothy must exercise faith in Jesus Christ as he retains and preaches these truths. This demanding charge cannot be carried out in Timothy's own abilities or strength. He is far too inadequate for this difficult task. This young preacher cannot be self-reliant and self-focused. He must have unwavering faith in Jesus Christ as he preaches the Word. He must look to Christ for the power to hold fast to the truth. He will be able to do so only as he walks closely with the Lord Jesus—he must abide in Him. As he does, there will be a divine enablement given to Timothy to retain this standard. Without it, he will never succeed in the mission to which God has called him.

As Timothy preaches the Word, he must firmly believe that Jesus will build His church (Matt. 16:18). He must have strong confidence that as he proclaims the truth, Christ will draw His sheep to Himself (John 10:27). As he expounds the riches of Scripture, he must have a sure trust in the Lord to open hearts to receive it (Acts 16:14). He must have the certainty that as he heralds the truth, Jesus will add to His church those who are being saved (Acts 2:47). He must believe that Jesus can convert His most hardened enemies according to His sovereign will (Acts 9:3–5). This is the unshakable reliance that Timothy must have in the Lord Jesus Christ as he proclaims this truth.

THE LOVE TO EXPERIENCE

Seventh, Paul concludes that Timothy must retain the truth "in the . . . love which [is] in Christ Jesus." In other words, this task must never be carried out in a cold, sterile manner. A dead orthodoxy will never succeed in pulpit ministry. Instead, as the standard of sound words is proclaimed, there must be a warmhearted affection for Jesus. Timothy must cultivate the fires of a blazing heart of love for Christ as he holds fast to the truth. This growing love for Christ will provide the high-octane motivation to endure in the Lord's work. He must pursue the love for Christ that is reflected in being kind to all and patient when wronged (2 Tim. 2:22, 24).

This quality of love (Gk., *agapē*) is self-denying and self-giving. It is the kind of love for Christ and others that can only come from

Jesus Christ. Such love is unconditional and unmerited, just as Jesus's love for Timothy is. It is not based upon the loveliness of the one loved, but upon the abundant supply of love that faith in Jesus Christ provides. This love is marked by personal sacrifice that gives in order to seek the highest good for another.

Paul wrote elsewhere about how absolutely necessary love is in the ministry of preaching the Word. He states, "If I speak with the tongues of men and of angels, but do not have love, I have become a noisy gong or a clanging cymbal" (1 Cor. 13:1). In other words, it does not matter how eloquent a man speaks if he is without love for Christ and the people to whom he preaches. If a man is without love, he is merely an empty noise. Timothy must speak the truth in love (Eph. 4:15). He must expound the Word with love for Christ Jesus. Only then will he have true love for the people he will minister to.

AN ENDURING CHARGE

This individual verse that we have examined is a key component in the farewell charge that Paul issued to his young protégé Timothy. To summarize, this young preacher must hold fast the truth that has been entrusted to him. He must not allow any deviation from this standard of sound words that he has heard from his father in the faith. But this strict retention cannot be carried out in his own strength. His preaching can only succeed by his continual faith in Jesus Christ. This trust will enable him to remain faithful to the divine truth. This charge must also be kept with love for Christ Jesus. A dead orthodoxy will be counterproductive and useless.

The standard Paul entrusted to Timothy extends to every preacher who stands in the pulpit before an open Bible. This same charge is issued to every minister who steps behind the sacred desk. All divinely appointed messengers must retain the standard of sound words. Simply put, there is a zero-tolerance policy for any departure from these doctrines. We are never to modify this immutable truth in order to accommodate the shifting times in which we live. On the last day, it will be a "stricter judgment" for teachers of the

Word (Jas. 3:1). This charge is sobering and straightforward.

NAIL YOUR COLORS TO THE MAST

Centuries ago, Britain fought many of its wars on the open seas of the Atlantic Ocean. Controlling the waterways was vital to the national security of the crown. British warships were required by international law to identify themselves by flying the colors of their sovereign. The British flag was to remain aloft the ship's mast at all times. If the national colors were ever lowered, it was the understood signal of the captain's unconditional surrender to the opposing side.

However, when the captain of the ship was determined never to surrender, he would give the order, "Nail the colors to the mast." At that command, an appointed sailor would climb the center mast and literally nail the Union flag to the mast. Once securely fastened, it could not come down. This bold move declared to the sailors on board that under no circumstances would they surrender the ship to the enemy. They must fight to the death and, if need be, the captain would go down with the ship.

This same irreversible commitment must embolden every preacher of the Word of God. In the midst of spiritual warfare, whenever the truth is under assault, he must be resolved to nail his colors to the mast. He is never to surrender the truth to the enemy. No matter what opposition is confronting him, the faithful herald of the gospel must retain the standard of sound words. He must be willing to face the assault of foes and, if need be, lose the support of friends before compromising sound doctrine. Ultimately, he should be willing to go down with the ship before he would surrender the truth.

HOLD FAST TO THE STANDARD

Every man of God who steps into a pulpit must wholeheartedly believe in the divine inspiration and inerrancy of the Word of God.

He must be fully committed its sufficiency. But there must be an even greater resolve in the depth of his soul. He must nail his colors to the mast and hold fast to the standard of sound words. No matter what stormy seas he encounters, he must retain the doctrine entrusted to him in the biblical text. He must be courageous in the face of threatening adversity. He must be willing, if need be, to go down with the ship. Under no circumstances of apparent defeat may he surrender the truth that has been passed on to him in the Word of God.

May God give every preacher persevering grace in the midst of the challenges confronting him. May every man of God encounter the many storms battering his pulpit ministry with unflagging resolve in order to retain the standard of sound words.

No.7

IN PRAISE OF GOD'S WORD

BY MARK DEVER

I remember bumping into Stephen Hawking when my wife and I lived in England. He was the Lucasian Professor of Mathematics at Cambridge University, a position he held for thirty years. He was a best-selling author and a celebrated theoretical physicist. For much of his life, he was considered one of the foremost minds in the world.

He and I met repeatedly during lunch in my years at Cambridge, maybe ten times. I say "met"—I mean we physically bumped into each other as we were trying to sit down at the long tables in the Grad Pad. I don't think I ever introduced myself, though we must have exchanged "Sorrys" nearly a dozen times. It was somewhat bizarre to have such a close, common experience with this man that I knew so much about, and yet really didn't know at all. It's strange bumping into a giant.

I think that's how some preachers feel about Psalm 119.[1] I think they look at it, and it looks really long and imposing. And they know it's great, but they just feel a little like they're bumping into a giant. Some are scared off by the sheer magnitude of it, and they retreat to Psalm 19 or Psalm 1 instead. For even the most seasoned shepherds and skilled exegetes, Psalm 119 is a daunting task. It could take months, even years to chart and explore the Bible's longest chapter, or to properly plumb its depths. Certainly the space available to me here is insufficient for a thorough study. But I believe we can do more than merely bump into the giant.

We ought to begin with a little background. We don't know who wrote it; some say it was David. Others believe that it is the work of the prophet Jeremiah. Some have suggested that it was the journal of a faithful Hebrew's reflections about the Word of God from the days of his youth on through the trials of midlife and older age, collected together at the end. While it could be a psalm of David, I believe it comes from later in Israel's history. It strikes me as the work of someone living in exile at a point when the Torah, God's law, had become freshly appreciated and valued by a people who no longer had the Temple available to them.

Whoever authored Psalm 119 did a masterful job of organizing it. The psalm is a work of artistic precision and creative genius. It is composed of 1,064 words in Hebrew, arranged in 176 verses in 22 stanzas—one stanza for every letter of the Hebrew alphabet. There are eight verses in each stanza, and each of those verses begins with that stanza's signature letter. The result is that each letter has its opportunity, as it were, to lead us in praising God for His law and His testimonies. All the letters are used to show that this praise is both full and complete. And yet, at the same time, it shows that the entire alphabet can be exhausted before we come to the end of the glories of God's law.

---

[1] Mark Dever read through the entirety of Psalm 119 when he preached this sermon at the 2015 Shepherds' Conference, just as he also did when he preached it to his congregation at Capitol Hill Baptist Church.

Today I don't think we're well prepared to fully appreciate what is going on in Psalm 119. We live in a culture of informality and spontaneity. We value the sincerity of the immediate and the casual. To us, that seems real, and therefore valuable. And we're just the kind of people—marked by our love for ease and convenience—who can miss the rich beauty in art. After all, artfulness and deliberateness show thoughtfulness. And in Psalm 119, we see the beauty of expression *itself*, reflecting something of the beauty being reflected upon.

Many Christians throughout church history have treasured this beautiful prayer. Some, like William Wilberforce, even memorized it and repeated it regularly. Many others recite it in part. Some have taken a single verse to meditate on every morning, and work steadily through the whole chapter twice a year. Space won't allow us the luxury of such intense and detailed study. Nonetheless, I pray God will give us more than a rushed tour of the Alps.

WHAT IS IT?

As we approach this biblical giant, several questions will help us understand and profit from this psalm. The first is simply a question of content: *What is God's law?* I think it is clear that the author has more in mind here than just the Ten Commandments.

The word "law" can have both narrow and broad meanings in the Bible. Sometimes it can refer to specific rules or a collection of rules. So the collection of rules that God gave to Moses must be at least part of what the author referred to here. That points us to Deuteronomy, where Moses summarized the law for the Israelites right before they entered the Promised Land. It's also possible that everything beginning from Mount Sinai (in Exodus 19) up through Deuteronomy might be in view.

However, the fact that some of the words used in this psalm are broader words—like "word" and "promise"—indicates that the psalmist here has in mind not only the whole Torah or the whole Pentateuch (the first five books of the Bible), but also all the other parts of God's Word the author would have known of. He seems to quote or at least make allusions to Isaiah, Jeremiah, the Proverbs, and other parts of God's Word. The variety of words used for God's law throughout the psalm—word, judgments, statutes, decree, law, commands, precepts, ways, promises—evidence this broader understanding. To put it simply, Psalm 119 is not talking about just the Ten Commandments, but about the whole of Scripture! This believing poet is reflecting on the relationship he has with God. And that relationship is possible only because God revealed Himself to His people in His commands, His decrees, His promises and statutes—His Word—to Abraham and Moses, to David and Isaiah.

God's Word has always been fundamental to the existence of His people. Of course, even the world itself was made by God's Word, as He spoke creation into existence, and it was by God's Word that Adam and Eve were created. God's Word of promise came to the Gentile Abraham and made him the father of the faithful, the progenitor of God's covenant people. God's Word came to Jacob, to Joseph, and to Moses down the centuries. Through Moses, God's Word established the nation of Israel; and through the leaders that followed from Joshua to David and beyond, God's Word led His people. Prior to and more fundamentally than the Temple, it was the Torah that shaped God's people and made them His. This is the Word, the commands and statutes that are being celebrated in this great psalm.

Israel's exile exposed the fundamental nature of God's Word, which had been obscured by human tradition. Then, with the coming of the Messiah, Jesus fulfilled the Law and the Prophets (Matt. 5:17). We see Christ's fulfilling work illustrated in the way He picked up the Passover meal, which was the meal of the Mosaic Covenant, and showed how it pointed to His own work and His own reign in the Last Supper (cf. Luke 22:14–20). He fulfilled all the Old Testament laws—civil, ceremonial, and moral. Nowhere is that more succinctly summed up than in the words of Christ Himself, as He quotes the Old Testament in Mark's gospel. "You shall love the Lord your God with all your heart, and with all your soul, and with all your mind, and with all your strength" (Mark 12:30), and, "You shall love your neighbor as yourself" (v. 31). And after Christ's ascension, He sent His Spirit to inspire and direct His apostles to reflect on the Old Testament and to use it to instruct the church in its infancy.

The law of God in view in Psalm 119 is the fullness of His self-revelation, spelled out across the expanse of His Scripture. The psalmist was praising God for the revelatory Word of God that was available to him at the time of his writing. We who live and serve after the completion of the biblical canon have all that much more to rejoice in and be thankful for.

WHAT IS IT LIKE?

Understanding the breadth of the psalmist's topic and the scope of his praise leads us to a second question, this one concerning the character of God's law. Specifically, we need to ask, *What is God's Word like?* If Scripture is God's revelation of Himself to us, what can we know about the quality and character of His revelation?

Here is where Psalm 119 becomes a solemn, joyful celebration as God's Word is revealed to be *true*, and *good*, and *everlasting*! Lose any one of those characteristics and Scripture would be greatly diminished, if not utterly defeated and destroyed. But with all three together, the future that would otherwise be dark and foreboding becomes flooded with glorious light.

To begin with, the psalmist assures us that God's Word is *true*. In verse 29, he contrasts God's ways with our false ways. In verse 142 he writes, "Your law is truth." Verse 151 echoes that thought: "All Your commandments are truth." And in verse 160 he concludes, "The sum of Your word is truth."

God has never spoken falsely—not to our first parents, and not to us. Our enemy Satan lies constantly. He attaches his lies to half-truths, and from the beginning, he has schemed to make God seem unfair, inconsistent, and deceptive. But God is nothing like that. He is always and only truthful. All His law is true, all

His commandments are true, and His promises never fail. He never misleads us. He never lies or tries to deceive us. Throughout Psalm 119, God's Word is shown to be unfailingly true.

Moreover, His Word is also *good*. Again and again, the psalmist proclaims that God's rules—His judgments and ordinances—are righteous (vv. 62, 75, 106, 160). His word of promise is righteous (v. 123, ESV). There is nothing wrong or questionable about the way He bestows salvation to His people by grace through faith in Christ. There is nothing wrong with the way He saved Abraham, the way He set aside Israel as His covenant people, and the way He rescues sinners from the due penalty of their sins. Reflecting on the goodness of God's Word, the psalmist cannot help but exclaim, "Your testimonies are righteous forever" (v. 144). Our hearts must echo his cry.

The church in the twenty-first century needs to lock this fundamental principle into our minds: God *defines* what is good. Goodness and righteousness are not some external standards that He effortlessly and perfectly conforms to; rather, goodness is a way of describing God and all of His actions and commands. "Good" is not determined by whoever happens to be sitting in the Oval Office, or the collective will of a legislative body. It's not determined by the number of one's Twitter followers, or what's fashionable at the moment. Down the street from Capitol Hill Baptist Church is a court that has, at one time or another, declared it legal that two men can marry each other, that infants in the womb may be killed, and that people can own each other like property. They are hardly the final arbiters of goodness!

So if it's not popularity, or electability, or legality, what is it that finally determines what is good? God does. And He has revealed it to us in His Word. "Seven times a day I praise You, because of Your righteous ordinances" (v. 164). If we are confused about what is right and wrong, we can simply look to God's Word, because all His precepts are right (v. 128). We don't have to worry about which instructions are accurate and which ones are not—the psalmist proclaims, "All Your commandments are righteousness"

(v. 172); "Your ordinances are good" (v. 39).

And all of this makes sense, because the character of God's Word reflects His character. The psalmist puts it briefly but beautifully in verse 68, "You are good and do good." What a wonderful, simple summary of praise to God.

But it gets even better—God's Word is also *everlasting*. The psalmist is not worried that this true and good Word will change, expire, or give out. The Bible will never need an update or a patch from the cloud. God's Word is "from of old" (v. 52), which is to say it is ancient. It is not a new thing. Describing God's testimonies in verse 152, the psalmist proclaims that God has "founded them forever." There is no sense that God's Word is failing, or that it will last any shorter than forever.

When it comes to mankind's words and actions, change is the order of the day. We are fickle, capricious, and unreliable—and we're accustomed to such inconsistencies in others. But God and His Word do not waver or change. As the psalmist says, "Every one of Your righteous ordinances is everlasting" (v. 160). In verse 89 he exclaims, "Forever, O Lord, Your word is settled in heaven." The Word of our Lord is eternal and unchanging. Put simply, it is everlasting.

Now it is true that when the psalmist wrote those words, God's special revelation of Himself through His Word had not yet concluded. Perhaps some of the Old Testament prophets were still to come. Certainly, the Lord Jesus Christ and His apostles had not yet come, nor had they taught and written what they would under the inspiration of the Holy Spirit. But none of those revelations changed what God had already revealed. The walls of the New Testament were to be built squarely on the foundations of the Old. Apart from the New Testament, the Old would have been incomplete. And without the Old, the New would make no sense. And with the full scope of God's revelation in view, we can affirm with the psalmist that there is no uncertainty or inconsistency with our heavenly Father—"All [His] commandments are faithful" (v. 86).

At this point the psalmist has led us into a wonderful celebration of praise. This is the Word of the one and only God, the eternal, unchanging, ever good, always true God. And the quality and character of the Word corresponds directly to the God whose Word it is. *He* is like this; He is truthful, and good, and eternal. Throughout this psalm the Word of God is identified very closely with God Himself. And you can understand why. His Word is His emissary, His ambassador. It is a revelation of Himself and His will and His character, His statements about the future in His promises, or about the past in His judgments. This is why, from the very beginning in verse 2, the psalmist emphasizes the parallel of keeping the Lord's testimonies with seeking Him. They reflect His character—they are like He is. "Righteous are You, O Lord, and upright are Your judgments" (v. 137). God is righteous, and His rules are righteous. They are like He is, in that they reflect Him through their truth.

Don't misunderstand what the psalmist is teaching here. The Bible is not God; but apart from the Bible, we cannot know God as we do. We can reflect on the world around us and know that it bears the marks of a Creator. And everyone will one day know God as his or her Judge. But if you want a relationship with God, there is no way for you to know Him apart from this Word. His written revelation is how He has made Himself known. Scripture gives us the best view of Him in His fullness. So to attack the Word of God is to attack God, and to honor the Word of God is to honor God.

Have you stopped to consider and appreciate what the Lord has given us in His Word? What a tremendous and invaluable resource it is. God's Word is here for us to understand what is true and good and unchanging. It exists for us to know Him and His will.

WHAT DOES IT DO?

We could draw many more implications about what God's Word is like from this great psalm, but we need to move on to our next question, this one having to do with operation: *What does God's Word do?*

Being the Word of the all-powerful God, we shouldn't be surprised to learn that God's Word is active, that it accomplishes things; it *does stuff*. Or, perhaps, it is better to say that God does stuff with His Word, by working through it in the lives of His people. Generally speaking, what God's Word does is bless. Look at the way our psalm begins: "How blessed are those whose way is blameless, who walk in the law of the Lord. How blessed are those who observe His testimonies, who seek Him with all their heart" (vv. 1–2). A blessed life is the natural result of knowing, loving, and obeying the Word of God.

The psalmist includes a kind of Aaronic benediction later in verse 135: "Make Your face shine upon Your servant, and teach me Your statutes." How would teaching someone God's statutes—His Word—be a means of blessing? In so many ways! Let me mention just five.

First, for those who believe the Bible, God's Word inspires awe. In verse 161 the psalmist writes, "Princes persecute me without cause, but my heart stands in awe of Your words." The emphasis is squarely on "Your words." Never mind those who threaten him with persecution, the author says he will fear and obey the Word of the Lord. Even when he could be occupied by other concerns—like simply staying alive—the writer confesses his steadfast commitment to God's Word. He says, "Seven times a day I praise You, because of Your righteous ordinances" (v. 164). And in verse 171, "Let my lips utter praise, for You teach me Your statutes." God's Word is awe-inspiring, causing His people to pray and to praise Him. It draws us into intimate fellowship and a right relationship with Him.

We can highlight a second blessing: God's Word causes us to grieve over our sin. It is clear that the psalmist took sin seriously. Look at verse 136, "My eyes shed streams of water, because they do not keep Your law." Or again, in verse 53, "Burning indignation has seized me because of the wicked, who forsake Your law." Studying God's Word does not make us morally indifferent. On the contrary, it educates our consciences, directing and sharpening them, and causes us to see this world and the people in it more like God does. If you want to cultivate a heavenly perspective on sin—and particularly, your own sin—become a faithful student of Scripture.

That connects to a third blessing: When we're faced with temptation, God's Word helps us to stay pure. Verse 9 has to be one of the best-known verses in this long psalm: "How can a young man keep his way pure? By keeping it according to Your word." And then look down a couple of verses to verse 11: "Your word I have treasured in my heart, that I may not sin against You." Do you have any doubt that God's Word encourages holiness? Consider the psalmist's confession, "I have restrained my feet from every evil way, that I may keep Your word. I have not turned aside from Your ordinances, for You Yourself have taught me" (vv. 101–102). The Word of God is the church's primary defense against temptation. We are fools if we fail to use it.

Remember how the Lord Jesus met temptation during His incarnation? He quoted the Bible to Satan. Our Savior leaned on the true and good and everlasting promises of Scripture as a defense against temptation. Do we dare presume that we have any less need to know and use the Bible than Christ did? If the Lord Jesus used Scripture to defend Himself from the lure of sin, why would we assume we could dispense with it? The Bible is a storehouse of practical helps we need to live faithfully as Christians—we must not ignore it!

Fourthly, God's Word is a blessing to those in need. To put it another way, God's Word gives hope to the hopeless. Over and over, the psalmist confesses that he is waiting on the Word of God, that his hopes are fixed upon it (vv. 43, 49, 81, 114, 147). He exalts Scripture as the great comfort for the afflicted (vv. 50, 52, 76). God's Word buoys the believer's heart through all the trials of life: "I have inherited your testimonies forever, for they are the joy of my heart" (v. 111). The Bible is a vast and precious treasure: "I rejoice at Your word, as one who finds great spoil" (v. 162). For all believers, and particularly those going through hard times, God gives peace through His Word. "Those who love Your law have great peace, and nothing causes them to stumble" (v. 165). He also provides the wisdom and insight required for faithful, righteous living: "From Your precepts I get understanding; therefore I hate every false way" (v. 104, cf. vv. 98–100). That is why it makes so much sense to conceive of the Bible as a kind of flashlight. The psalmist paints that very picture in verse 105: "Your word is a lamp to my feet and a light to my path." And again in verse 130: "The unfolding of Your words gives light; it gives understanding to the simple."

You realize that is what should be happening right now. As you are reading and reflecting on God's Word in Psalm 119, His Holy Spirit who inspired its writing is causing light to shed in your mind and heart. By the Spirit's work through the Word, you are pushing past the veil of sin and self-deception and perceiving realities in a way that is more akin to the truth. Through the work of the Word, God is answering prayers that you may have prayed in humility to have better understanding, better judgment, and deeper wisdom—prayers like the one in verse 66: "Teach me good discernment and knowledge, for I believe in Your commandments." Psalm 119 is effectively one long prayer, full of several small prayers to the Lord to teach us His Word and to open our eyes. In verse 27 the author pleads with God, "Make me understand the way of Your precepts." And in verse 73, "Give me understanding, that I may learn Your commandments." It's clear that Psalm 119 is not a call to pull yourself up by your spiritual bootstraps.

God's Word is learned only by God's gift. And we need to faithfully pray about our own study of His Word and our reliance on Him. In fact, prayer is more valuable and more important than all the commentaries in your library. I remember my uncle telling me long ago that a crucial part of Bible study that too many Christians omit is simply but sincerely asking God to reveal Himself to us in His Word. We must not commit the careless sin of approaching this Book in a purely academic sense. We need to get in the habit of pleading with the Lord to help us know Him by knowing His Word better every day.

I love how the psalmist puts it in verse 24: "Your testimonies also are my delight; they are my counselors." Are you taking the Bible as your trusted counselor in life? Or have you found a lot of other books that are easier and more to the point of what you're looking for? It's significant that throughout Psalm 119, the psalmist both trusts God and asks God to help him trust Him more. We cannot ignore the obvious help that God's Word is.

In fact, the most amazing thing God gives us through His Word is life. Verse 50: "Your word has revived me." We need to faithfully consider the testimony of God's past goodness. In verse 93 the psalmist says, "I will never forget Your precepts, for by them You have revived me." His Word is the means He uses to give us spiritual life. Our local church has as our church motto, "Faith comes by hearing." It's taken from Romans 10:17, "Faith comes from hearing, and hearing by the word of Christ." That's the only way someone ever is saved from their sins and reconciled to God—by hearing that great message that the eternal Son of God took on flesh and lived a life of perfect obedience, and then died a death He did not deserve. Apart from Scripture, we would never know that Christ took that death in our place as a substitute for all of us who would turn from our sins and trust in Him. We wouldn't know that God raised Him from the dead or that He ascended to heaven, signifying that the Father accepted the sacrifice of His Son. Apart from Scripture, we would not hear His call to repent and believe. God's Word offers hope to the hopeless. In fact, His Word is their only hope.

Finally, a fifth blessing: God's Word brings deliverance to those in trouble. The psalmist knew what it meant to be in trouble. But he knew just as well that God's Word promises deliverance (v. 170), help (v. 175), and, as we've just seen, salvation (v. 41). In the face of trials and trouble, God's people must look to His everlasting Word for help, strength, and comfort.

Those five blessings offer us only the briefest glimpse into what God's Word does in the lives of His people. There is much more we could mine from Psalm 119, but we must not miss what the psalmist says about the nature of the Word, because it so wonderfully reflects the nature of the God who spoke it. The quality and character of Scripture reflect its Author, and we ought to be grateful for the insight we receive from this glorious psalm.

HOW SHOULD WE RESPOND?

At this point, one question remains. We have seen what God's Word is like—that it is true, good, and everlasting. We've also considered what it does, and specifically some of the ways God uses it to bestow His blessings. Now we simply need to ask the question of correlation: *How should we respond?* The psalmist spells out five basic responses in his magnificent prayer.

First and most obviously, we should obey God's Word. The psalm begins by extolling the blessings for those who obey the Lord. Obedience is a theme repeated again and again throughout the psalm (cf. vv. 55–56, 112, 117). God gives His people life by His Word. Why would anyone think we weren't also called to believe and obey it? The psalmist points to that correlation in verse 88, "Revive me according to Your lovingkindness, so that I may keep the testimony of Your mouth." No small part of God's reason for giving us new life is that we would, as the author puts it in verse 115, "Observe the commandments of my God." Our basic response to the Word of God should be obedience.

We should also love it. The psalmist conveys this important response to God's Word in so many ways, not the least of which is the sheer intricacy of the way he's designed and laid out the psalm in the first place. He also speaks directly and at length to how we are to delight in Scripture. In verse 14 he writes, "I have rejoiced in the way of Your testimonies, as much as in all riches." "I shall delight in Your statutes; I shall not forget Your word" (v. 16). In verse 35 he prays, "Make me walk in the path of Your commandments, for I delight in it" (cf. vv. 24, 70, 77, 92, 143, 174). He extolls the greatness of God's Word in verse 129, "Your testimonies are wonderful; therefore my soul observes them." God's Word should be sweet to His people: "How sweet are Your words to my taste! Yes, sweeter than honey to my mouth!" (v. 103). We should long for it, as he describes in verse 131, "I opened my mouth wide and panted, for I longed for Your commandments." It should be invaluable to us: "The law of Your mouth is better to me than thousands of gold and silver pieces" (v. 72), and "I love your commandments above gold, yes, above fine gold" (v. 127).

Is that your testimony? Can you agree with the words of the psalmist? Can you echo his confession, "I shall delight in Your commandments, which I love" (v. 47)? Our lives ought to reflect the kind of love for Scripture the author describes in verse 167, "My soul keeps your testimonies, and I love them exceedingly."

Third, we should respond to God's Word by meditating on it. The psalmist exclaims in verse 97, "O how I love Your law! It is my meditation all the day." Verse 148 makes it sound like he rose early in the morning just to spend more time dwelling on God's Word: "My eyes anticipate the night watches, that I may meditate on Your word." He sang it, too: "Your statutes are my songs" (v. 54) and, "Let my tongue sing of Your word, for all Your commandments are righteousness" (v. 172). The hymns we sing at Capitol Hill Baptist Church deliberately reflect the psalms. They are often thick with biblical content and allusions, quoting Scripture and emphasizing key doctrines to help us remember God's Word. I have been with many saints near the end of their lives, when their memories are failing, but by God's grace they can remember the hymns they have sung. Many young Christians have memorized verse 11, "Your word I have treasured in my heart, that I may not sin against You" (cf. vv. 93, 109, 141). Whether you read it, listen to it, pray it, memorize it, or sing it, make a habit of meditating on the Word of God.

A crucial part of obeying, loving, and meditating on God's Word is another response: trusting it. In verse 42 the psalmist writes, "I trust in Your word." And he was wise to do that. We encounter many people in this life whose words we cannot trust, nor should we. But you can always trust God. His Word is always worthy of our trust. Verse 90 tells us His "faithfulness continues throughout all generations." God is faithful, and so is His Word. So we can count on it, knowing it won't let us down. Verse 140 is one of my favorite in the chapter: "Your word is very pure, therefore Your servant loves it." Who knows all the trials the psalmist had faced? He endured physical challenges, having enemies, being despised, dealing with criminals and immoral people, oppression—those and many others he mentions in the psalm. God's promises were likely well tested over the life of the psalmist, and each time they were proven faithful and true.

Reflecting on your own life for a moment, do you have similar reason for confidence in the promises of God? Has the faithfulness and reliability of His Word been proven over and over in your life? We need to remember that God's Word is faithful and true, and we need to trust in His promises.

Finally, in addition to obeying and loving, meditating on, and trusting in God's Word, there is one other crucial response we must not neglect. Rightly responding to Scripture means we must also fear the God whose Word it is. We can't overlook the words of verse 120, "My flesh trembles for fear of You, and I am afraid of Your judgments." God's Word brings us into a kind of contact with God Himself. And by His grace, this contact wakes us up spiritually. As we begin to understand more of good and bad and wrong and right, we begin to appreciate more of how we've been bad and wrong, and how in God there is only what is good and what is right. We're able to recognize the moral distance between our Creator and us. Moreover, we begin to see that this is the God who will judge us. And when that understanding first dawns in a person's heart, it can be deeply disorienting, jarring, and frightening. And even after we come to hear and believe the gospel, we're left with a profound sense of the difference that remains between a righteous God and us. We understand something of His holiness and our unworthiness, which makes us regard both Him and His Word with genuine respect and trembling gratitude, as we marvel at His love and mercy toward us.

Psalm 111:10 says, "The fear of the Lord is the beginning of wisdom." If we're truly going to obey and love God's Word, and if we're going to faithfully meditate on it and trust it, we must begin with holy fear and awe for God Himself. Put simply, we can't respond to God's Word appropriately if we don't properly respond to Him.

A NEW TESTAMENT VIEW OF PSALM 119

Our brief exploration of Psalm 119 would be incomplete if we failed to note that the psalmist is not just talking about the Bible, or the written Word of God. Some people in Jesus's day seemed to believe that the psalm was that narrowly defined. But the sinner's true way home—the end of our exile, the completion of this exodus, isn't fundamentally through our obedience to God's written Word. Instead, our true deliverance comes through the Word made flesh, who perfectly obeyed in our place. We need to understand that it does not dishonor God's written revelation to say that it points to something greater than itself. As the author of Hebrews writes, "God, after He spoke long ago to the fathers in the prophets in many portions and in many ways, in these last days has spoken to us in His Son" (Heb. 1:1–2). John's gospel begins with a similar emphasis. "In the beginning was the Word, and the Word was with God, and the Word was God. . . . And the Word became flesh, and dwelt among us, and we saw His glory, glory as of the only begotten from the Father, full of grace and truth" (John 1:1, 14).

It isn't that we don't obey God's Word; we do obey it genuinely, but imperfectly. And our lives are being genuinely but imperfectly circumscribed by the law of God, giving evidence that we have truly trusted in the One whose life was perfectly circumscribed by the Word of God—the One who bestows His righteousness to us as a gift. And it is the gift of perfect righteousness through Jesus Christ that this psalm so wonderfully points to again and again.

Consider again how the psalm begins. "How blessed are those whose way is blameless, who walk in the law of the Lord. How blessed are those who observe His testimonies, who seek Him with all their heart" (Ps. 119:1–2). Whose way has been more blameless, who more faithfully and wholeheartedly sought to do His Father's will than Jesus Christ, the Son of God? And who fulfilled it more perfectly? Twice the Father said to the disciples that He was well pleased with His Son (Matt. 3:17, 17:5). Our psalm rightly proclaims blessing on such a one. And surely, more blessed than anyone who has ever lived should be the life of the only One who perfectly, blamelessly walked in the law of His Father and sought Him with His whole heart!

But that's not what happened to Jesus. No. In fact, His death by crucifixion is called "cursed" by the very law He perfectly fulfilled (Deut. 21:22–23). What an irony that the only One who perfectly kept the law was wrongfully condemned and killed as a lawbreaker.

Christ taught His disciples that His death was prophesied again and again in the Old Testament. After He rose from the dead He told His disciples, "All things which are written about Me in the Law of Moses and the Prophets and the Psalms must be fulfilled" (Luke 24:44). And what was written about the Word made flesh in Psalm 119?

Reading the psalm with New Testament eyes, it is virtually impossible to miss the foreshadowing of the person and work of Christ. The psalmist's words drip with details alluding to the One who called Himself the Servant of the Lord, who even as a young boy said He must be about His Father's business (Luke 2:49). In Psalm 119:99–100 we read, "I have more insight than all my teachers, for Your testimonies are my meditation. I understand more than the aged, because I have observed Your precepts." Regarding the One who wept over Jerusalem's rejection, verse 136: "My eyes shed streams of water, because they do not keep Your law." Of the One who overturned tables in righteous anger at the sin that consumed the temple courts, verse 53: "Burning indignation has seized me because of the wicked, who forsake Your law."

Certainly Christ faced the kind of fierce opposition described in verse 110, "The wicked have laid a snare for me," and verse 95, "The wicked wait for me to destroy me." He could have easily identified with the words of verse 157, "Many are my persecutors and my adversaries, yet I do not turn aside from Your testimonies."

Do you hear echoes of Gethsemane in verse 143? "Trouble and anguish have come upon me, yet Your commandments are my delight." Or how He suffered for righteousness' sake, only to be smeared with lies: "The arrogant have forged a lie against me" (v. 69)? Do you see Herod and Pontius Pilate in the affirmation that "princes persecute me without cause" (v. 161), or that "the cords of the wicked have encircled me" (v. 61)?

Or consider this mournful plea of the persecuted servant:

> Though I have become like a wineskin in the smoke,
> I do not forget Your statutes.
> How many are the days of Your servant?
> When will You execute judgment on those who persecute me?
> The arrogant have dug pits for me,
> Men who are not in accord with Your law.
> All Your commandments are faithful;
> They have persecuted me with a lie; help me!
> They almost destroyed me on earth,
> But as for me, I did not forsake Your precepts. (vv. 83–87)

Who could have more accurately claimed to be "exceedingly afflicted" (v. 107), or more safe in the knowledge that "in faithfulness You have afflicted me" (v. 75)? Who could have confessed, "I have inclined my heart to perform Your statutes forever, even to the end" (v. 112), if not the One who cried out on the cross, "It is finished!" (John 19:30)—the One who was utterly forsaken that we might not be so.

And who better could have cried out, "Hear my voice according to Your lovingkindness; revive me, O Lord, according to Your ordinances. . . . Look upon my affliction and rescue me, for I do not forget Your law. Plead my cause and redeem me; revive me according to Your word" (Ps. 119:149, 153–154)? From where could that be prayed more truly than from the tomb of Christ?

And, of course, the Lord did give Him life. And through the sacrifice and resurrection of the Word made flesh, He gave life to all who come to trust in Him. And so we are, as Psalm 119 begins, truly and abundantly blessed in Christ, who was both cursed and blessed in our place.

Praise God for His Word!

No.8

EVANGELICALS, THE CHALLENGE OF MODERNITY, AND THE QUEST FOR A CHRISTIAN WORLDVIEW: Lessons from a Century of Hope and Disappointment

BY R. ALBERT MOHLER, JR.

"All that is solid melts into air." That was the confident boast of Karl Marx in the first chapter of *The Communist Manifesto*, written in 1848. Marx's confidence was that everything that represented the authoritative pillars of Western society would dissolve in the spirit of modernity and revolution, and that religion—most importantly, Christianity—would dissolve into thin air. The "opiate of the people" would simply disappear, and no one would miss it.

Clearly, history did not unfold as Karl Marx and Friedrich Engels predicted. Their promised Communist Age never appeared, and the worldwide workers' revolution did not happen. But it did turn out that the modern age would melt just about everything in its path. Western Europe is almost thoroughly secularized. The towers of medieval cathedrals stand as silent witnesses over cities inhabited by millions of thoroughly secular people living comprehensively secular lives. For the vast majority of Europeans, Christianity has receded so far into the historical background that it is no longer a part of the intellectual or moral consciousness. By the end of the twentieth century, Europe would commonly be identified as "post-Christian."

The same is true in North America, where Canadian culture tracks Western Europe's secularization very closely. Cities like Toronto are now virtually as secular as Prague and Amsterdam. The United States, long believed to be the exception to the rule, is becoming secularized in its own way and on its own timetable. Vast millions of Americans identify as Christians or claim some other form of theism, but the binding authority of biblical Christianity evaporates before our eyes. The American model of secularization, it turns out, has not followed the European example of overt secular hostility followed by theistic surrender. Instead, Americans, including millions of Americans who believe themselves to be Christians, have simply allowed the near-total evacuation of Christian truth and the binding authority of the Bible from their lives and minds. Vast megachurches dot the landscape, but in many of those giant auditoriums, little biblical content is to be found. Americans have allowed their hearts and minds to be secularized, even as they continue to attend church events and consider themselves Christians of some sort.

Peter Berger, the most influential American sociologist to observe the twentieth century, revised his theory of secularization accordingly. In the United States, he argued, secularization worked out to be a process of pluralization. Among the intellectual elites, the European model of open hostility to theism held sway. The faculty of Harvard University is as secular as the faculty of the Sorbonne. But for the greater population, people stayed in the pews while their basic worldview became pervasively secularized. In Europe the pews were evacuated. In the United States, many pews remained filled, but the Christian faith was evacuated. It turns out that solid can melt into air in more than one way.

Charles Taylor, the Canadian philosopher who has most thoroughly diagnosed the modern age, points out that even the fact of theistic belief is not the same in the wake of modernity. "To put the matter in different terms," he wrote, "belief in God isn't quite the same thing in 1500 and 2000."[1] In terms similar to Berger, Taylor underlines the fact that in the year 1500, people believed in God because the entire background of their lives demanded it as a reflex. In the year 2000, even those who believe in God have the sense that they have chosen this belief.

Behind all of this was a vast transformation in Western societies that is best identified as modernity: the emergence of the modern age and the comprehensive reshaping of the intellect, human life, and social structures. Modernity is represented by the massive shifts of mind that would include the Enlightenment, the rise of modern science, a pervasive attitude of doubt, the liberalization of morality, and the subversion of natural social structures, including marriage and the family. Modernity promises liberation, and anything or anyone that stands opposed to it is recast as the enemy of human liberation. Biblical Christianity becomes the villain, an obstacle that must be overcome.

Thoughtful Christians have perceived this new situation with alarm and concern. How will Christians remain faithful to Christ, hold to the truths revealed in Holy Scripture, raise their children in the nurture and admonition of the Lord, and live authentically Christian lives in secularized cultures? The answers do not come easily.

But thoughtful Christians have also had to think carefully about *thinking*. When God is denied and revealed truth is despised, how can Christians remain true to Christianity?

THE EMERGENCE OF WORLDVIEW AS EVANGELICAL CONCERN

The concept of worldview is itself a product of the Enlightenment. The notion of a comprehensive view of God, humanity, and the world was not necessary when Christian theism dominated the landscape. Christianity provided the only accessible

---

[1] Charles Taylor, *A Secular Age* (Cambridge: Harvard University Press, 2007), 19.

worldview. This does not mean that all of the people who lived in areas dominated by the Christian worldview were Christians. It does mean that their picture of the world and their understanding of the biggest issues of life were drawn from Christianity. For most of Western history, there was simply no alternative.

The Enlightenment changed all that. By no coincidence, the most significant of the Enlightenment philosophers, Immanuel Kant, may have been the first to articulate the reality of a worldview, a *Weltanschauung*. As the Enlightenment and subsequent intellectual movements continued, the idea of a worldview became unavoidable, precisely because modernity offered the promise of new ways of knowing the world and our place within it.

Among English-speaking Christians, the first real argument for a Christian worldview came from Scottish theologian James Orr, in his book *The Christian View of God and the World*, first published in 1893.[2] By the time Orr wrote the book, theological liberalism and secular modes of thinking had presented conservative Christians in the United Kingdom with a massive challenge. He understood that the challenge to Christianity was total and comprehensive. Accordingly, Christians would have to make certain that their own belief systems were truly Christian. Thus, Orr urged believers carefully and strategically to embrace a worldview—"the widest view which the mind can take of things"—in order to remain intellectually Christian.[3]

In the Netherlands, Dutch Reformed theologian, journalist, and statesman Abraham Kuyper was attempting a similar project. The future Dutch prime minister visited Princeton University in 1889 to deliver the Stone Lectures, eventually published as *Lectures*

---

[2] James Orr, *The Christian View of God and the World* (Grand Rapids: Eerdmans, 1954). The first time I met Dr. Carl F. H. Henry, a towering evangelical figure of the twentieth century, he told me to read this book by James Orr. Henry had been introduced to the concept of a Christian worldview as a student at Wheaton in the 1930s, and had understood it through reading Orr's book.

[3] Ibid., 3.

on Calvinism.[4] Kuyper, deeply engaged in political life and social issues, went far beyond Orr in not only calling for a Christian view of God and the world, but arguing how such a worldview would take shape in various arenas of human thought and work, from the academy, to the government, and to the arts.

It was no accident that theologians such as Orr in Scotland and Kuyper in the Netherlands were far ahead of their Christian brothers and sisters in the United States. Living in the UK and in Europe, they felt the heat of modernity's challenge earlier and had to think faster. In the United States, conservative Christians of the early twentieth century would be far more concerned about fighting theological liberalism within the mainline denominations. The liberals won in almost all of the major mainline denominations and conservatives largely withdrew into new denominational structures or some form of congregational independence.[5]

At the same time, the dual cataclysms of the fight against Nazism and the looming Cold War against Communism would galvanize Christians to think about the great ideological challenges of the epoch. Closer to home, evangelical parents were aghast as they came to know the ideological forces that were competing for the hearts and minds of their children, especially on the campuses of premier colleges and universities. The idea of a *Weltanschauung* would appear with energy in a 1943 presidential address to the

[4] Abraham Kuyper, *Lectures on Calvinism* (Grand Rapids: Eerdmans, 1931). I read Kuyper's lectures as a college student upon the recommendation of Pastor D. James Kennedy, who would also introduce me, in print and in person, to Francis Schaeffer. Kuyper's lectures were my first exposure to the idea that theology was not just about the knowledge of God, but also about the knowledge of the world. It says a great deal about the state of evangelicalism in the US in that era, that the books most influential among many seriously minded Christians had been written by theologians in Scotland and the Netherlands almost a century earlier. American evangelicals were late to see the challenge of modernity, and overly pragmatic in their response to it.

[5] The Southern Baptist Convention, never listed among the "mainline" denominations that dominated the North and the American establishment of the era, would experience its own version of a battle over theological liberalism roughly a half-century after the controversies in the mainline denominations. In the Southern Baptist conflict, the conservatives eventually won. In retrospect, the issues of the 1920s in the North and the 1970s in the SBC were eerily parallel.

National Association of Evangelicals by Boston pastor Harold John Ockenga. "We are standing at the crossroads," Ockenga declared, "and there are only two ways that lie open before us. One is the road of the rescue of western civilization by a re-emphasis on and revival of evangelical Christianity. The other is by a return to the Dark Ages of heathendom, which powerful force is emerging in every phase of world life today."[6]

While other leading evangelical figures such as Carl F. H. Henry would also write extensively about the need for and the defense of the Christian worldview, the mainstream evangelical concern for the concept would come after the cultural crises of the 1960s had broken onto the scene, and the figure who would be most identified with the concept in the evangelical mind was Francis A. Schaeffer.

Schaeffer, whose theology was forged in the mid-century theological conflicts within American Presbyterianism, would go with Edith, his wife, to Switzerland to establish a missionary outpost directing disaffected students and other young people. The center became known as L'Abri, and Schaeffer soon developed a reputation for engaging the culture as a thinking Christian. Schaeffer's first major speaking tour in the United States did not come until 1965, but he quickly became the most influential advocate for the development of a Christian worldview among believers, applied to every dimension of life and thought.

By the end of the twentieth century, American evangelicals were in general agreement on the need for a Christian worldview and on the urgency of devoting time and energy to such development. A veritable library of books and a universe of conferences and seminars and academic programs emerged. Oddly enough, the German word *Weltanschauung*, translated as *worldview*, had become a central component of the evangelical vocabulary and the

---

[6] Harold John Ockenga, "Christ for America," Presidential Address to the National Association of Evangelicals, in *United . . . We Stand: A Report of the Constitutional Convention of the National Association of Evangelicals, May 3–6, 1943* (Boston, NAE, 1943) cited in Molly Worthen, *Apostles of Reason: The Crisis of Authority in American Evangelicalism* (New York: Oxford University Press, 2014), 26.

evangelical mind in the United States.

The explanation for this development is quite simple. Evangelicals would develop and defend a Christian worldview, or all would be lost. Without Christian thinking, founded on biblical truth, there is no Christianity.

WORLDVIEWS IN COLLISION

The state of the evangelical mind on the importance of worldview is exemplified by philosopher Ronald H. Nash's 1992 book, *Worldviews in Conflict: Choosing Christianity in a World of Ideas*.[7] Nash, who would influence a wide audience through his teaching on the faculties of Western Kentucky University, Reformed Theological Seminary, and The Southern Baptist Theological Seminary, defined worldview as "a set of beliefs about the most important issues in life."[8] He continued:

> The philosophical systems of great thinkers such as Plato and Aristotle were worldviews. Every mature rational human being . . . has his or her own worldview just as surely as Plato did. It seems sometimes that few have any idea what that worldview is or even that they have one. Yet achieving awareness of our worldview is one of the most important things we can do to enhance our self-understanding, and insight into the worldviews of others is essential to an understanding of what makes them tick.[9]

Nash would argue that a worldview is a "conceptual scheme by which we consciously or unconsciously place or fit everything we

[7] Ronald H. Nash, *Worldviews in Conflict: Choosing Christianity in a World of Ideas* (Grand Rapids: Zondervan, 1992).

[8] Ibid., 16.

[9] Ibid.

believe and by which we interpret and judge reality."[10] Accordingly, "Instead of thinking of Christianity as a collection of theological bits and pieces to be believed or debated, we should approach our faith as a conceptual system, as a total world-and-life view."[11] He cited William J. Abraham to make this point:

> Religious belief should be assessed as a rounded whole rather than taken in stark isolation. Christianity, for example, like other world faiths, is a complex, large-scale system of belief which must be seen as a whole before it is assessed. To break it up into disconnected parts is to mutilate and distort its true character. We can, of course, distinguish certain elements in the Christian faith, but we must still stand back and see it as a complex interaction of these elements. We need to see it as a metaphysical system, as a worldview, that is total in its scope and range.[12]

Nash then proceeded to advocate for an understanding of being, truth, logic, and reality that is drawn from and consistent with biblical truth. Beyond this, he engaged rival worldviews in an attempt to deepen understanding and to underline the superiority of the biblical truth-claims and the Christian worldview. Other authors would take a similar course, with many extending the argument to how Christians should understand and engage not only the unavoidable questions of truth, but the various dimensions of culture, from music and the arts to politics, history, economics, and psychology. Christian colleges, with greater and lesser success, sought to engage or to "integrate" the Christian worldview with academic disciplines. An array of seminars and books sought to

---

[10] Ibid.

[11] Ibid., 19.

[12] William J. Abraham, *An Introduction to the Philosophy of Religion* (Englewood Cliffs, NJ: Prentice-Hall, 1985), cited in Nash, 20.

help Christians develop a Christian worldview and apply it to their lives, their studies, their professions, their consumer decisions, and their understanding of media and entertainment.

What could go wrong?

CHRISTIAN WORLDVIEW: THE CRITIQUE

The critique of the worldview emphasis that emerged in the late twentieth century was largely driven by more liberal rejections of evangelical theology. Some argued that the evangelical vision of a Christian worldview was intellectually insufficient, which usually meant insufficiently accommodated to the prevailing secular mind. Others argued that the evangelical concept was too narrow, especially if based upon the inerrancy of Scripture and the exclusivity of the gospel of Christ. To most conservative evangelicals, these criticisms had little effect. In fact, for many evangelicals the criticisms from the left merely served to underline the importance and urgency of the conservative project.

There is the criticism offered by figures such as Molly Worthen of the University of North Carolina, who has not been reluctant to offer an indictment of conservative Christianity. In *Apostles of Reason: The Crisis of Authority in American Evangelicalism*, Worthen argues that American evangelicals, trying to hold onto biblical authority and cultural influence at the same time, turned to the worldview project as a defensive response to modernity and as an effort to influence the culture—even to save civilization. By her description, evangelicals turned the worldview project into an effort to change the culture, especially through conservative moral change. Looking at the last decades of the twentieth century, Worthen argued: "Evangelicals' long-running debate over biblical authority was now a battle for civilization—and they needed to act while there was still time."[13] Worthen's history of evangelicals on these issues is important, and she is right to point to the

[13] Worthen, 216.

unwarranted optimism of the New Christian Right, as it was called. But her critique of the worldview project, though thoughtful, offers no sympathy for conservative Christians seeking to remain faithful to biblical Christianity in the modern age.[14]

More recently, there have been other lines of critique. James K. A. Smith, professor of philosophy at Calvin College, has offered a major critique in his book, *Desiring the Kingdom: Worship, Worldview, and Cultural Formation*, published in 2009.[15] Smith argued that the worldview approach is reductionistic and misdirected. According to his indictment, the concern for worldview among Christians has been too intellectualistic, too cognitive. In his view, Christianity (and Christian education in particular) is primarily *formative* and not *informative.*

In his words,

> how we think about distinctly Christian education would not be primarily a matter of sorting out which Christian ideas to drop into eager and willing mind-receptacles; rather, it would become a matter of thinking about how a Christian education shapes us, forms us, molds us to be a certain kind of people whose hearts and passions and desires are aimed at the kingdom of God.[16]

Such an approach, he argues, is "going to require that Christian education find its font and its foundation in the practices of Christian worship."[17] His approach is more about liturgy than apologetics.

---

[14] Worthen has offered her critique of my own thought in this book and elsewhere. I am honestly thankful for thoughtful criticism, but in the end my concerns for Christian faithfulness override concerns about the judgment of the culture. Furthermore, the evangelical project may indeed fail, but Christ's church will not fall.

[15] James K. A. Smith, *Desiring the Kingdom: Worship, Worldview, and Cultural Formation* (Grand Rapids: Baker Academic, 2009).

[16] Ibid., 18.

[17] Ibid., 18–19.

A similar critique has been offered by James Davison Hunter of the University of Virginia. He argues that evangelical Christians have based their worldview project on a backward understanding of how ideas and culture relate. Evangelicals, he warns, think that intellectual change produces cultural change. They are wrong, he asserts. Cultural change produces intellectual change. The exchange of *ideas* comes after, not before, the change of cultural *practices*.[18] In other words, evangelicals have been overconfident that they can change—even transform—the culture through winning the society to Christian ideas, even doctrinal content and morality. Hunter's own project would require a more comprehensive rethinking of evangelical Christianity in America, but the important dimension of his critique is found in the similarity of his main point to the concern he shares with James K. A. Smith.

Is this critique justified? Without doubt, Smith and Hunter have important points to make. The evangelical project of the Christian worldview can be, and often is, overly cognitivist and intellectualist. Smith's argument is deeply Augustinian in his insistence on a more comprehensive understanding of Christian education, culture, and the formation of Christians. Furthermore, no biblically minded Christian can argue against the priority of worship over any other Christian endeavor.

And yet, this critique seems to fail on three counts. First, because it fails to account for the conflict of ideas that will not remain on pause or go dormant during the long and ultimately most important process of Christian formation. Issues and ideas demand attention now, and will not wait. This points to the second problem, which is the failure to acknowledge the urgency of apologetics in the contemporary cultural and intellectual context. The third problem is the context of theological confusion in the

[18] James Davison Hunter, *To Change the World: The Irony, Tragedy, and Possibility of Christianity in the Late Modern World* (New York: Oxford University Press, 2010). I have offered a lengthier engagement with this book by Hunter in R. Albert Mohler, Jr., "To Change the World?," in *Revisiting 'Faithful Presence':* To Change the World *Five Years Later*, edited by Collin Hansen (Chicago: The Gospel Coalition, 2015), 81–88.

church today. Christians cannot avoid dealing with hard questions about biblical truth, and some form of a worldview project is unavoidable in this light.

In the end, it is difficult to understand the overt hostility to the worldview project that Smith and Hunter, as illustrations, offer here. Indeed, one suspects that they actually participate in some form of the worldview project themselves. Perhaps their critique is partially explained by Smith's liturgical reflex and Hunter's social environment at the University of Virginia. In any event, evangelicals can learn from the critiques, but are left with the urgency to develop and defend a Christian worldview and to transmit it to the next generation of Christians.

But how?

RETHINKING THE WORLDVIEW PROJECT: THE PRIMACY OF EXPOSITORY PREACHING

The great surprises of my adult life have been the velocity of the challenge of modernity, on the one hand, and the persistence of superficial Christianity, on the other. Nothing in the modern onslaught has really surprised me, but the velocity of secularization continues to amaze me. Just to think of one example, consider the cultural shift on the questions of same-sex marriage and the transgender revolution. Whereas in previous ages such vast moral changes would require centuries, they now happen within single decades or even less.[19] Add to this the realization that open hostility is now coming swiftly to Christians who hold to doctrine and moral beliefs that Christians have held universally through two millennia.

But the second surprising fact, which has amazed me, is the persistence of superficial Christianity. Logic would indicate that

---

[19] See R. Albert Mohler, Jr., *We Cannot Be Silent: Speaking Truth to a Culture Redefining Sex, Marriage, and the Very Meaning of Right and Wrong* (Nashville: Thomas Nelson, 2017).

this cannot last, for under conditions of social hostility, one would expect superficial Christian identity and participation to evaporate. But it has not. At least, not yet. Once again, Peter Berger seems to have seen the future. His theory that the American form of secularization would take the shape of pluralization from within the churches (and even within individuals) seems to hold here. Cultural Christianity simply makes its peace with modernity, requiring only the continuation of outer forms and some vague "spirituality" or vacuous theology. Same-sex marriage? No problem. Everything is negotiable, and the strategy of accommodation returns, virtually unchanged from when the Protestant liberals used it decades earlier.

And where are all of those Christians who have attended the millions of hours of worldview seminars? Where are all the graduates of the colleges and universities who pledged to uphold the Christian worldview? Where is the evidence of cultural advance? What did the evangelical worldview project produce, anyway?

At this point, the question must be turned to theology and away from sociology. If we are looking for sociological or cultural evidence, we will be disappointed. If we were betting on cultural dominance, we will be devastated. If we thought that individuals would keep thinking like Christians if they are not truly Christians—regenerate, faithful disciples of the Lord Jesus Christ—we were fooling ourselves.

So, what are we left with? Well, we are left with everything that God in Christ has promised His church. We are left with the gospel. We are left with the Bible. We are left with the blessed hope. We are left with the knowledge that the gates of hell shall not prevail against Christ's church.

That is good news, and it is enough. The evangelical worldview project, rightly understood, was never about producing people who would think like Christians. It was about teaching Christians to believe the truth of God's Word, to be able to apply that Word to their lives and thoughts, to be faithful in every dimension of their lives.

There is nothing wrong with seminars, books, lectures, and massive educational efforts. They all have their place. None of them, however, is the means by which God has promised to form Christians into faithfulness.

Preaching is.

The maturation of Christian believers occurs in the context of the church, and by the ordinary means of grace. And the central means is the exposition of the Word of God. The fact that this turn in this argument takes some people by surprise underlines the current crisis. Far too many evangelicals think that Christians can be conformed to Christ by merely thinking Christian thoughts. This is not God's promise. God promises to conform believers to the image of Christ through the ministry of the Word. The preaching of the Word, the exposition of Holy Scripture, verse by verse and text by text and book by book is the means Christ uses to build His church. Christians are formed in the church through the preaching of the Word of God, as the Holy Spirit applies that Word to the hearts and minds of believers in a way that no mere human means can reach.

The priority of expository preaching in the New Testament, building upon the ministry of the Word in the Old Testament, is abundantly clear. No one reading the New Testament can miss it.

So what is rightly at the center of Christian worship? The reading and preaching of the Word of God. What does God use to build Christian believers into faithfulness? The preaching of the Bible. How is the mind, regenerated by God, reshaped into alignment with God's truth? By the ministry of the Word.

Is there a place for seminars, video series, books, and authentically Christian colleges and universities? Of course there is. Is our ultimate confidence in any of them? No, surely not. Then what is even more important? The preaching of the Word to Christ's people in churches ordered by Scripture.

When I was invited to write a chapter for a volume honoring John F. MacArthur on fifty years of ministry at Grace Community

Church, these thoughts came together firmly. In one man, in one ministry, in a half-century of faithful exposition, we see the relentless proclamation of God's Word to the men and women of a single congregation—and through them to millions of others. Through the entire span of the history of the evangelical project to develop and defend the Christian worldview, John MacArthur has been doing so by preaching, one verse at a time, through the Bible.

Over time, when the Bible is rightly preached, everything needful happens. God uses the preacher to read the text and to explain it, to answer every big question of life, and to confront every moral issue and deal with every apologetic challenge. That is how Christians are made, and that is how the Christian worldview takes possession of hearts and minds.

Of all people, Karl Marx had the first word in this essay: "All that is solid melts into air." He was confident he was right.

But let the last word be from the prophet Isaiah in response: "The grass withers, the flower fades, but the word of our God stands forever" (Isa. 40:8).

No.9

THE FOLLY OF ADDING TO SCRIPTURE

BY CONRAD MBEWE

The preservation of the Bible through history is unquestionably a miracle. Efforts to destroy it have come from all sides, but each of them has failed. Some sought to silence God's Word by destroying every copy they could find. Others attempted to stifle its influence by hindering its translation into everyday language, sequestering Scripture to archaic languages like Latin. More recently, those who are intent on assaulting Scripture have sought to undermine its credibility as the inerrant and inspired Word of God. They insist that the Bible is full of inaccuracies and errors, and therefore it cannot be trusted. But in the last one hundred years, a much subtler assault on the truth has emerged and risen to prominence—an attack on Scripture's *sufficiency*.

This is not an entirely new idea, but a version of an ancient lie that has exploded in popularity over the last century. This latest attack comes from those who have no problem with the Bible being available for anyone who wants to read it. They also support its translation into the languages of unreached people all over the planet. In fact, they will even defend Scripture from anyone who suggests that the Bible is full of errors, because they believe it is the inspired Word of God. However, they also firmly believe that God still speaks today, personally revealing His will to His people. The result is a Bible that is inspired but *insufficient*, as they see the need for God to add to Scripture by continuing to reveal Himself in the way He did to the Old Testament prophets and to the New Testament apostles and prophets.

In a real sense, these implicit doubts about the sufficiency of Scripture are what God warned believers about at the end of the last book of the Bible. The apostle John writes,

> I testify to everyone who hears the words of the prophecy of this book: if anyone adds to them, God will add to him the plagues which are written in this book; and if anyone takes away from the words of the book of this prophecy, God will take away his part from the tree of life and from the holy city, which are written in this book. (Rev. 22:18–19)

John was the last of the apostles—men that Jesus Christ, the Son of God, directly chose to lead and teach His church after His return to heaven, and to write much of the New Testament. John penned these words of warning while exiled on the island of Patmos, at a time when the church was under intense persecution. On Patmos, God commanded him to write to the churches the visions and words that now constitute the book of Revelation.

Revelation tends to be difficult to understand, due in part to its requirement that the reader have a good grasp of the Old Testament in order to fully apprehend what John wrote. That was deliberate. John wanted to encourage the church through what he was writing, and at the same time keep his message hidden from those intent on persecuting believers. The church would have been familiar with the Old Testament Scripture, but the persecutors would not. But one thing is clear: The book of Revelation was to be the last authoritative message from God. Its closing words are carefully written to ensure that this message is loud and clear. The words of Revelation 22:18–19 are a warning to all who would read John's final letter to the churches. It was a warning that spelled out in equally clear detail what would happen to those who did not heed it.

THE FINAL WARNING OF THE APOSTLE JOHN

The words of warning were delivered in between two invitations. In verse 17 John writes, "The Spirit and the bride say, 'Come.' And let the one who hears say, 'Come.' And let the one who is thirsty come; let the one who wishes take the water of life without cost." It is not immediately clear who is being encouraged to come in the first part of the verse. Is it the Lord Jesus (see vv. 7, 12, and especially 20, where Jesus says He is coming soon), or is it the person who is thirsty (see v. 17b)? What is clear is that the second part of this verse serves as an invitation to those who are listening or reading the words to come to Christ, the water of life, and find salvation for their souls. Another invitation in verse 20 bookends the text: "He who testifies to these things says, 'Yes, I am coming quickly.' Amen. Come, Lord Jesus." Through John, Christ assures the readers that He is coming back. And the apostle John himself longingly says, "Come, Lord Jesus!" With that, there is only the final benediction (v. 21) before the entire book of Revelation comes to an end. These, then, are some of the final words of the Bible, and the very last words from God to His people.

In between these invitations or overtures, we have the words of warning. There is nothing in this chapter or its immediate context to prepare the reader for this warning. It is not part of the development of any thought. It simply stands out in bold relief in the midst of positive words of longing. What exactly was John warning about?

Some people think that John was simply warning those who would be copying this book for further distribution not to add their own words or remove any words from the biblical text. In the New Testament world, the process for copying and circulating written works was laborious. There were no typewriters or printing presses—it was all handwritten. Individuals had to meticulously copy word for word what was written in the original. Often, in order to create multiple copies, one person would read the original aloud while a group of writers simultaneously recorded what they heard. For that reason, some argue that John was simply warning those who would be copying these words to do so with extreme caution. He was urging them not to carelessly add to or subtract from what was written. That is understandable—the message of this book was divinely inspired, and should be conveyed to believers in various regions and to coming generations with integrity and consistency. However, the weakness with this view is that John's warning is to "everyone who hears the words of the prophecy of this book," and not only to copyists. The warning is to the end user—the hearer. It is to all, even today in the computer era, where this book is on tablets and on phones. All receive the same urgent warning not to add to or subtract from this book.

So another explanation is needed. What exactly was John warning the readers about? It seems that the answer is found when one contrasts these words with a promise that was made earlier in the chapter. In verse 7, John said that the Lord Jesus told him, "And behold, I am coming quickly. Blessed is he who heeds the words of the prophecy of this book." Notice the parallel with verses 18–19. In both cases the words are couched in promises of Jesus's coming. Also, both of them have to do with "the words of the prophecy of this book." In the earlier verse, readers are promised blessings if they keep "the words of the prophecy of this book," while the closing verses threaten punishment for those who add to or take away from those words.

That contrast sheds light on what the apostle John is saying here. He is simply echoing the word of Jesus, amplifying them by putting them in a negative light. John is saying that the responsibility of God's children is to obey what God has said—not to assume that

God has left out something else that He ought to have said, and thus add to His revelation. God's people also are not to assume that part of what God has said is unnecessary, and thus overlook those aspects of His revelation. Both extremes are wrong. Believers must build their lives squarely on the foundation of what God has said—in its entirety.

It is difficult to read the words of Revelation 22:18–19 without concluding that the book of Revelation closed the canon of God's authoritative Word to His people. In his book *Understanding Spiritual Gifts*, Robert L. Thomas says,

> The conclusion of this investigation accepts the inevitability of connecting the decline and cessation of the spiritual gift of prophecy to Revelation 22:18. Compliance with, indeed universal knowledge of, this warning was not immediate. Nevertheless the divine intention behind the warning necessitated that it eventually be recognized and that the body of Christ move into new phases of its growth without dependence on the foundational gift of prophecy.[1]

God's people need to consider the weightiness of the phrase "if anyone adds to [the words of the prophecy of this book], God will add to him the plagues which are written in this book." Imagine belonging to a local church in the New Testament era and hearing those words read aloud. Would you not think twice about presuming that you could legitimately stand up in the congregation of God's people and add what you think are God's words developing in your mind? Even if the gift of prophecy was not withdrawn immediately, surely such an ending to the final book from the pen of the last surviving apostle would suggest that the extraordinary gift of prophecy was seeing its last days. I cannot see it any other way.

---

[1] Robert L. Thomas, *Understanding Spiritual Gifts: A Verse-by-Verse Study of 1 Corinthians 12–14*, second ed. (Grand Rapids, MI: Kregel Publications, 1999), 153.

RECENT CLAIMS TO THE GIFT OF PROPHECY

Throughout its history, the Christian church has taught that ongoing revelation was necessary while the foundation of the first-century church was being laid. There were truths about Christ that needed to be revealed because they lay hidden in the Old Testament. These truths needed to be uncovered and explained to the church—work which the Lord accomplished through the inspired writings of the apostles and the prophets under their leadership. The New Testament is the compilation of that written revelation. The church still stands on that foundation laid two thousand years ago.

Paul described the Lord's revelatory work in his letter to the Ephesians.

> For this reason I, Paul, the prisoner of Christ Jesus for the sake of you Gentiles—if indeed you have heard of the stewardship of God's grace which was given to me for you; that by revelation there was made known to me the mystery, as I wrote before in brief. By referring to this, when you read you can understand my insight into the mystery of Christ, which in other generations was not made known to the sons of men, as it has now been revealed by His holy apostles and prophets in the Spirit; to be specific, that the Gentiles are fellow heirs and fellow members of the body, and fellow partakers of the promise in Christ Jesus through the gospel. (Eph. 3:1–6)

Paul speaks about this "mystery" that was made known to him by revelation. The word "mystery" here is not referring to something indiscernible, but rather to truth that was once hidden and has now been revealed by God. That is how Paul himself defined it; he said it was that "which in other generations was not made known to the sons of men, as it has now been revealed by His holy apostles and prophets in the Spirit" (v. 5). In this case, the mystery is about Christ and the plan of God to make Gentiles equal partners with the Jews in His kingdom in this New Testament church.

Notice how Paul is very clear whom the channels of this revelation are: "[God's] holy apostles and prophets." He wrote earlier that these apostles and prophets were the foundation of the New Testament church: "So then you are no longer strangers and aliens, but you are fellow citizens with the saints, and are of God's household, having been built on the foundation of the apostles and prophets, Christ Jesus Himself being the corner stone" (Eph. 2:19–20). Once a foundation is laid, the next step is to erect a superstructure on it. One does not continue laying a foundation forever. God gave His direct revelation to the apostles and prophets so that with it, they could lay the foundation of the New Testament church. The foundation has been fully laid. Believers now are to build on it by simply preaching this revelation until Jesus Christ returns.

What is the witness of history to this truth? The church has always declared that the Scriptures are inspired, authoritative, and infallible. However, the sufficiency of the Scriptures has remained a point of contention between Protestants and the Roman Catholic Church. The Catholic Church teaches that God has spoken through Scripture *and* tradition. By tradition, they mean the pronouncements made by popes and councils through history. The Reformers fought against the supposed authority of man-made tradition, arguing that God has spoken to His people through His Word alone. The watchword for that doctrinal position was *sola Scriptura*, and it meant that only that which is found between Genesis and Revelation carries divine authority to bind the consciences of the people of God. The Reformers understood that the words of men cannot be elevated to equality with the Word of God. As Martin Luther explained during his trial at the Diet of Worms, mere men—even popes and church fathers—frequently contradict one another. Clearly, they can't all be speaking for God.

It was not long after the Protestant Reformation that documents like the Westminster Confession of Faith were composed to state unequivocally, "The whole counsel of God concerning all things necessary for his own glory, man's salvation, faith and life, is either expressly set down in Scripture, or by good and necessary consequence may be deduced from Scripture: unto which nothing at any time is to be added, whether by new revelations of the Spirit, or traditions of men."[2] That God's Word is both sufficient and complete has been a hallmark of Protestant theology since the Reformation.

In the centuries since, there have been times when self-proclaimed prophets have claimed to bring fresh revelations from God, inevitably resulting in the formation of a cult. The Church of Jesus Christ of Latter-Day Saints is one case in point. It was founded by Joseph Smith, Jr., who claimed to receive visions and prophecies from God. To this day his followers, the Mormons, see him as a prophet on the same level as the Holy Spirit-inspired human authors of the Bible—regardless of the fact that his teachings contradict the clear and consistent testimony of God's Word. Another example are the Seventh-Day Adventists, founded by Ellen G. White. She claimed to have been a prophetess who received over two thousand dreams and visions from God to pass on to His people. And while her supposed revelations from God emphasized a religion of works that contradicts what Scripture teaches about justification by faith alone through grace alone, her followers equate her writing with God's Word.

Orthodox Christianity always maintained a clear distinction from those who made such claims. Those who persisted in stressing the validity of new revelation were excommunicated, or left the church to launch their own cults. However, things changed at the start of the twentieth century with the explosion of the Pentecostal movement within the evangelical church. Many people saw it as the restoration of the apostolic gifts, with particular emphasis on speaking in tongues, prophecy, and healing. In mere decades, the Charismatic movement grew exponentially in influence, becoming one of the dominant trends in the evangelical church. What was once held in suspicion and rightly condemned as unbiblical has

[2] The Westminster Confession of Faith, Chapter 1, Paragraph 6.

now gained widespread acceptance throughout the visible church. And in spite of its public affirmation of Scripture's sufficiency, evangelicalism is now overrun by those claiming to be prophets and apostles who hear directly from the Lord.

BELIEVING THE SUFFICIENCY OF SCRIPTURE

The moment the church allows for the continuation of such revelatory gifts, it is declaring that Scripture is insufficient for belief and practice. We are saying that we need more.

God Himself has given His people a book that is adequate to supply all that they need. The apostle Peter wrote, "His divine power has granted to us everything pertaining to life and godliness, through the true knowledge of Him who called us by His own glory and excellence. For by these He has granted to us His precious and magnificent promises, so that by them you may become partakers of the divine nature" (2 Pet. 1:3–4). So through the knowledge of God, which He has provided in His Word, the church has all that it needs—"His precious and magnificent promises" in Scripture which, when applied to individual lives, enable growth from one degree of glory to another. Put simply, it is the Word of God alone that the Holy Spirit will use to save and sanctify God's people. He has not promised to use any other words. Jesus prayed to the Father, saying, "Sanctify them in the truth; Your word is truth" (John 17:17). It is God's inspired Word that He would use to sanctify His people. So why do professing believers want anything more?

Just before his martyrdom, the apostle Paul wrote to his protégé Timothy, "All Scripture is inspired by God and profitable for teaching, for reproof, for correction, for training in righteousness; so that the man of God may be adequate, equipped for every good work" (2 Tim. 3:16–17). Paul was essentially telling Timothy that everything he needed to lead the souls of his congregation heavenward was abundantly supplied in God's Word. Through the Scriptures that were breathed out by God, Timothy was completely equipped for every good work. What more could he want or need?

It is a well established fact that John MacArthur has championed the cause of the sufficiency of Scripture. He has stated that "*sola Scriptura* simply means that all truth necessary for our salvation and spiritual life is taught either explicitly or implicitly in Scripture."[3] Through the precepts, the principles, and the precedents that abound in the Bible, God's people can learn everything they need for the salvation and sanctification of their souls. The role of preachers is not to come up with more of God's revelation. Rather, it is to explain and apply what God has already revealed in the Scriptures.

THE FOLLY OF INSISTING ON ONGOING REVELATION

There are at least three reasons it is utter folly to insist on—or even to leave the door of possibility open to—ongoing revelation from God outside of the first century. The first might simply be called the folly of failing to learn from history. It has been said that the only lesson we learn from history is that we never learn from history. There is ample evidence throughout church history that this is true—particularly when individuals in the church have claimed to receive fresh revelation from God. We already noted the founding of the Church of Jesus Christ of Latter-Day Saints and the Seventh-Day Adventists; countless other cults were founded on the spurious teaching of men and women claiming to hear from God. In fact, there is not a single movement born from such claims that has resulted in stable spiritual growth and doctrinally sound churches. It's a tragically well-trod path that consistently leads to theological chaos and spiritual disaster. Today, with the widespread acceptance of extrabiblical revelation in evangelicalism because of the Pentecostal and Charismatic movements, Pandora's box has been opened, and countless men and women have been led astray by false teachers claiming to speak for God.

---

[3] John F. MacArthur, Jr., "The Sufficiency of the Written Word" in *Sola Scriptura: The Protestant Position on the Bible*, edited by Don Kistler, (Morgan, PA: Soli Deo Gloria), 165.

Second, there is also the folly of surrendering Scripture's authority. Whenever individuals have added to Scripture, Scripture has inevitably taken second place while the addition has become the primary focus. It is the "extra" revelation that consistently becomes the center of attention. It is like the tale of the Arabian camel that first pushed its head into its master's tent. When the master allowed the camel the space for its head, it soon pushed in its shoulders. Slowly but surely, it pushed its way farther in until the master found himself crowded out of the tent altogether. New revelation always seems more glittering compared to the Bible that everyone is already acquainted with—inviting fresh revelation always makes the established Word of God seem stale by comparison. Moreover, accepting new revelation often breeds pride and vanity. Those supposedly receiving the revelation expound their own dreams and visions more and more, because it distinguishes them and their followers from everyone else. Inevitably, Scripture takes second place while the new revelation becomes supreme. There is no better way to subvert the authority of God's Word than to invite new revelation into the church.

Finally, there is the folly of inviting confusion. Once we allow for fresh revelation beyond the closure of the canon, it becomes impossible to settle controversy. False teachers will point to their own pronouncements as words from God, with no fixed standard to measure them against. Some churches collapse into warring factions over contradictory revelations; others drown in the conflicting messages, unable to discern the difference between God's Word and those who pretend to speak for Him today. In the days of the apostles, those chosen men were the final arbiters in controversy. From the earliest days of the church, false prophets have claimed to speak for God, often bringing teaching that flatly contradicted the teaching of the apostles. That is why God's chosen men wrote the Holy Spirit-inspired truth in their epistles—they faithfully recorded what they knew to be the very mind of Christ (1 Corinthians 2:13). And while the apostles don't weigh in on controversies today, we have the record of their teaching, and the truth they used to confront error (often the same error prevalent today). But if the canon is not closed—if God is still speaking through all the people who claim to hear from Him today—how does the church discern truth from error? How can it settle doctrinal controversy if its opponents can point to other writings and teachings from people who can lay equal claim to being prophets and apostles? Evangelicalism's openness to ongoing revelation has unleashed doctrinal confusion and chaos on a global scale.

In light of all that, it is the height of human arrogance for anyone to imagine that they have something to add to the inspired and authoritative Word of God. Those who do are effectively saying that the Creator of the universe and Author of history failed to communicate everything He intended—that *they* are necessary to pass along something He forgot or neglected to include in His Word.

Worse still, it leaves believers with a God who contradicts Himself. He has said we are adequately equipped through His inspired Scripture (2 Tim. 3:17). He has even made it clear that we should not add anything to "the words of the prophecy of this book" (Rev. 22:18). Should we really believe that He then goes on to speak directly through more and more prophets across the rest of history?

Instead of trying to add to Scripture, let us be encouraged by what Revelation 22:7 says: "Blessed is he who heeds the words of the prophecy of this book." Our job is not to add or subtract, but to keep the words that have already been spoken by God, both in the book of Revelation and throughout the rest of His Word. God promises that we will be blessed when we do so. Our families will be blessed, our churches will be blessed. Above all, He will be glorified.

No.10

WE MUST OBEY GOD RATHER THAN MEN:
Scripture, Authority, and the Reformation

BY NATHAN BUSENITZ

It was October, 1517, when a German monk in the town of Wittenberg posted a list of nearly a hundred arguments against the sale of indulgences. That document, first written in Latin, was soon translated into the German language. Thanks to Gutenberg's printing press, invented seven decades earlier, the 95 Theses circulated like wildfire. With passionate precision, Martin Luther gave voice to the protests of countless people suffering under the systemic corruption of medieval Roman Catholicism. It was unacceptable and indefensible, Luther argued, to hawk certificates of forgiveness as a fundraising campaign for church building projects. Many throughout Saxony agreed. The resulting groundswell sparked the sixteenth-century Reformation, with an emphasis on purifying the church and recovering the gospel.

But the roots of the Reformation reach back much earlier, and go down far deeper, than a solitary protest against a single corrupt practice. As the Protestant movement continued to gain momentum, the Reformers' fundamental focus centered on the issue of authority. Their primary concern might be phrased in the form of a question: Who is the head of the church? If the pope were the head of the church, then Christians ought to submit to papal decrees and church traditions as upheld by the Roman Catholic magisterium. But if Christ alone is the head of the church, as the Reformers contended, then Scripture alone stands as the final authority for faith and practice. Church traditions must be measured in light of the supreme authority of Scripture, being adjusted or even discarded when they contradict biblical truth.

Martin Luther singled out the issue of papal authority with these words:

> The chief cause that I fell out with the pope was this: the pope boasted that he was the head of the church, and condemned all that would not be under his power and authority. . . . Further he took upon him power, rule, and authority over the Christian church, and over the Holy Scriptures, the Word of God; [claiming that] no man must presume to expound the Scriptures, but only he, and according to his ridiculous conceits; so that he made himself lord over the church.[1]

In rejecting papal authority, the Reformers sought to obey God and His Word rather than the traditions and edicts of men. Fifteen hundred years earlier, the apostle Peter boldly declared to the religious leaders of Jerusalem: "We must obey God rather than men" (Acts 5:29). The Reformers echoed that same unflinching conviction. As the pre-Reformer John Hus (d. 1415) explained in his work *On the Church*:

> If the papal utterances agree with the law of Christ, they are to be obeyed. If they are at variance with it, then Christ's disciples

[1] Martin Luther, *The Table Talk of Martin Luther*, trans. and ed. by William Hazlitt (London: Bell & Daldy, 1872), 203–4.

> must stand loyally and manfully with Christ against all papal bulls [decrees] whatsoever and be ready, if necessary, to endure malediction and death. When the pope uses his power in an unscriptural way, to resist him is not a sin, it is a mandate.[2]

The Reformers insisted that Christ alone, not the pope, is the head of the church. Consequently, His Word alone is the final authority for His church. Moreover, the gospel articulated in that Word is the true gospel—the good news that sinners are justified by grace alone through faith alone based on the work of Christ alone. Conversely, the sacramental synergism of Roman Catholic tradition ought to be rejected because it runs contrary to biblical teaching.

When the Reformers compared the traditions of medieval Roman Catholicism with biblical teaching, they rightly rejected those which did not measure up to the standard of divine truth. Such unbiblical traditions included the veneration of Mary, prayers to the saints, indulgences, purgatory, mandatory celibacy of priests, auricular confession to a priest, compulsory fasts (like Lent), required tithes, and a sacramental system of works righteousness. These and other unbiblical traditions, like papal supremacy, characterized the Roman Catholic system. By elevating such extrabiblical beliefs and practices above the Word of God, the Roman Catholic Church had slipped into apostasy, allowing religious tradition to eclipse biblical truth.

SCRIPTURE VS. TRADITION

The Reformers stood resolute in the conviction that Scripture must be obeyed above all other authorities, including the pope and church tradition. They taught that, insofar as tradition runs contrary to biblical teaching, Christians are duty bound to submit to the

---

[2] John Hus. Cited from Matthew Spinka, *John Hus' Concept of the Church* (Princeton, NJ: Princeton University Press, 1966), 121.

Word of God above all else. This is the essence of the Reformation doctrine of *sola Scriptura* (Scripture alone).

Though a number of biblical passages could be cited in support of this doctrine (e.g. Acts 17:11; 2 Tim. 3:16–17; and others), one key text is Mark 7:1–13. In this passage, the Lord confronted the extrabiblical traditions of the Pharisees and scribes. In so doing, He unequivocally established the priority of God's Word above the religious traditions of men.

The theme of authority, specifically the authority of Christ, permeates Mark's gospel. This is evident in the sections immediately preceding Mark 7:1–13. In Mark 6:33–44, Jesus demonstrated His creative authority by miraculously feeding a crowd of five thousand men, plus women and children. In Mark 6:45–52, He exhibited authority over the elements, walking on water and calming a storm with a simple command. Mark 6 ends (in verses 53–56) by recording the Lord's authority over infirmity and disease, as He immediately and completely healed the sick who were brought to Him.

The buildup to Mark 7:1–13 highlights the authority of Christ and His Word. He prayed food into existence, commanded a storm into submission, and rebuked disease into remission. In each case, the created order submitted perfectly to the will and word of its Creator. Those examples stand in stark contrast to the obstinate unbelief of the religious leaders described in Mark 7. While the creation yielded fully to Jesus's authority, the Pharisees and scribes persisted in their rebellion against Him.

Consider the first 13 verses of Mark 7:

> The Pharisees and some of the scribes gathered around Him when they had come from Jerusalem, and had seen that some of His disciples were eating their bread with impure hands, that is, unwashed. (For the Pharisees and all the Jews do not eat unless they carefully wash their hands, thus observing the traditions of the elders; and when they come from the market place, they do not eat unless they cleanse themselves; and there are many other things which they have received in order to

> observe, such as the washing of cups and pitchers and copper pots.) The Pharisees and the scribes asked Him, "Why do Your disciples not walk according to the tradition of the elders, but eat their bread with impure hands?" And He said to them, "Rightly did Isaiah prophesy of you hypocrites, as it is written:
>
> 'This people honors Me with their lips,
> But their heart is far away from Me.
> But in vain do they worship Me,
> Teaching as doctrines the precepts of men.'
>
> Neglecting the commandment of God, you hold to the tradition of men."
>
> He was also saying to them, "You are experts at setting aside the commandment of God in order to keep your tradition. For Moses said, 'Honor your father and your mother'; and, 'He who speaks evil of father or mother, is to be put to death'; but you say, 'If a man says to his father or his mother, whatever I have that would help you is Corban (that is to say, given to God),' you no longer permit him to do anything for his father or his mother; thus invalidating the word of God by your tradition which you have handed down; and you do many things such as that."

This showdown between the Lord Jesus and the religious leaders unfolds like a courtroom drama. At the outset, the scribes and Pharisees act like prosecuting attorneys, eager to point out the violations committed by Jesus's disciples. In the end, the religious leaders are put on trial and condemned. As the narrative unfolds, Christ exposes the Pharisees' artificial system of tradition, contrasts it with the authoritative standard of Scripture, and reveals the appalling symptoms of a system that elevated tradition above the Word of God.

AN ARTIFICIAL SYSTEM OF TRADITION

Mark 7 begins with the scribes and Pharisees lodging a complaint against Jesus's disciples based on their artificial system of legalistic tradition. As self-appointed referees of first-century Judaism, the religious leaders were incensed to see their traditional rules being ignored and broken. Infuriated, they rushed to the scene of the alleged crime, eager to confront the violation.

On this occasion, the specific offense involved a failure to follow the proper protocols for ceremonial handwashing (see vv. 1–2). Modern sensibilities (about germs and the benefits of soap) might initially be inclined to sympathize with the Pharisees' complaint. But the concerns of the religious leaders had nothing to do with personal hygiene. They took offense, instead, because Jesus's disciples had not followed the ritualistic washings that were part of their rabbinic tradition.

In Leviticus 22:6–7, the law of Moses prescribed a type of ceremonial washing for those who were part of the priestly line of Aaron. But what the Old Testament designated only for priests, the religious leaders expanded into an elaborate ritual required for everyone. According to historian Alfred Edersheim, the traditional washing of hand purification involved several steps. Water was first poured over both hands with the palms pressed together and the fingers pointing upward. That step was repeated with the fingers pointing down. Then, one hand would make a fist. The pouring continued as that fist was rubbed in the palm of the other hand. This step was subsequently repeated with the other fist.

As Mark explains in verses 3–4, these ritualistic washings were part of the ceremonial cleansing that all first-century Jewish people were mandated to observe. For example, after returning home from the market, elaborate washings were deemed necessary to avoid ceremonial uncleanness (since it was possible to have become unclean while at the market). The impetus for this and other burdensome practices did not come from Scripture. It came from the religious traditions of the elders. And the scribes and Pharisees were eager to enforce these extrabiblical customs.

What were the traditions of the elders? They consisted of oral traditions and rabbinic rituals passed down from generation to generation, dating back to at least the time of the Babylonian Captivity (in the 6th century BC). Even today, adherents to Judaism look not only to the Old Testament Scriptures but also view the Talmud as authoritative. The Talmud includes those oral traditions along with rabbinic commentary on them. These traditions were originally created to safeguard the teaching and practices of the Mosaic law. But as they continued to grow, becoming more and more complex over the centuries, they eventually obscured the truth of the Scriptures they were invented to protect.

So, it was on the basis of tradition, not biblical command, that the Pharisees incredulously asked Jesus, "Why do Your disciples not walk according to the tradition of the elders, but eat their bread with impure hands?" Their motive was not one of curiosity, but derision and outrage. Like hypocritical hall monitors, they pounced when they saw Jesus's disciples eating with hands that had not been properly rinsed.

The religious leaders were right that a serious violation was being committed. But ironically, they were wrong about what that violation was and who was committing it. They assumed Jesus's disciples were guilty because they had ignored the traditions of the elders. In reality, the Pharisees were the transgressors because they prioritized religious tradition above the Word of God.

THE AUTHORITATIVE STANDARD OF SCRIPTURE

In the opening verses of Mark 7, the religious leaders played the part of prosecuting attorneys, seeking to trap Jesus by bringing charges against His disciples. They based their complaint on an artificial system of religious tradition. In verses 6–9, the Judge of the universe exposed their hypocrisy and the erroneous presupposition on which it was built.

Often throughout His ministry, the Lord came into conflict

with the religious leaders of Israel. The tragic reality is that the group who should have been most ready to receive Him as Messiah and Lord, actually responded to Him with rejection and hatred. As the apostle John wrote, "He came to His own, and those who were His own did not receive Him" (John 1:11).

On this occasion, Jesus cut to the heart of the matter. He countered religious tradition by appealing to a higher court of authority: the Word of God. He condemned the religious leaders based on the authoritative standard of Scripture.

> And He said to them, "Rightly did Isaiah prophesy of you hypocrites, as it is written: 'This people honors Me with their lips, but their heart is far away from Me. But in vain do they worship Me, teaching as doctrines the precepts of men.' Neglecting the commandment of God, you hold to the tradition of men." He was also saying to them, "You are experts at setting aside the commandment of God in order to keep your tradition."

Citing Isaiah 29:13 where the Lord indicted Old Testament Judah for their religious duplicity, Jesus rebuked these first-century leaders for their hollow legalism. Like the hypocrites of Isaiah's day, the scribes and Pharisees looked religious on the outside. On the inside, however, they were indifferent and even hostile toward the Word of God. Thus, they worshiped God with their lips, but their hearts were cold and distant.

If they had been true worshipers, they would have prioritized divine commandments over rabbinic rituals. They would have sought to obey God rather than men. Instead, in their legalism, they made much of external adherence to ceremonial customs while ignoring those things that truly please the Lord. The Pharisees and scribes created elaborate sets of external rules, and judged others accordingly. At the same time, they ignored the truth of God's Word—rejecting the very criteria by which God evaluates the hearts of men. Israel's leaders got their priorities backward. Instead of elevating the Word of God above their traditions, they fastidiously clung to their customs to the neglect of biblical truth. Tragically, they led the people under their influence to do the same.

The Lord Jesus responded by condemning them for their misplaced priorities. In so doing, He established the principle that God's Word is the authority over religious tradition. Consequently, tradition must yield to Scripture, not the other way around.

AN APPALLING SYMPTOM OF HYPOCRITICAL RELIGION

Having rebuked the religious leaders for their hypocrisy, Jesus provided an example of the bizarre extremes to which people can go when they prioritize man-made tradition over the Word of God. The example Jesus gave provided irrefutable evidence of the bankruptcy of the entire system. His words in verses 10–13 delivered a stinging rebuke:

> For Moses said, "Honor your father and your mother"; and, "He who speaks evil of father or mother, is to be put to death"; but you say, "If a man says to his father or his mother, whatever I have that would help you is Corban (that is to say, given to God)," you no longer permit him to do anything for his father or his mother; thus invalidating the word of God by your tradition which you have handed down; and you do many things such as that.

The Mosaic law instructed the Israelites to honor their parents (Ex. 20:12; 21:17). Yet rabbinic tradition had created an elaborate system in which basic biblical commands, like the Fifth Commandment, could simply be sidestepped.

By using this example, Jesus highlighted a conflict between God's Word and the religious traditions of first-century Israel. The biblical command is clear: Children are called to honor their parents by what they say and do. The implication is that they will continue to show proper love and respect, even as their parents grow old and begin to need care. But rabbinic tradition had created a loophole that enabled adult children to avoid assisting their aging parents. According to the tradition of the elders, a person could pronounce the word "corban" (a Hebrew word meaning "devoted to God") over his possessions, thereby reserving those possessions for eventual donation to the Temple. Once an asset was designated as "corban," it could not be sold or given away to anyone else.

This loophole allowed self-serving children to freeze their assets to the neglect of their aging parents. A person could use the term "corban" to lock down personal property so that he did not have to share his possessions, even with his aging parents. Conveniently, the "corban" declaration could later be reversed. After his elderly parents died, the child could regain full access to all of his assets without actually having to give anything to the Temple.

The potential abuses in such a system are obvious. But it illustrates the kind of corruption that can creep in when man-made tradition supersedes divine truth. The religious leaders allowed a rabbinic custom (the practice of labeling something as "corban") to override a clear biblical command (the responsibility children have to honor their parents). Neglecting aging parents to horde personal property is a contemptible act of selfish greed. To do so while claiming devotion to God is even more despicable. Yet Israel's leaders made allowances for such injustices because they prioritized the traditions of men over the Word of God.

In verse 13, Jesus nailed the coffin shut: "[You are] invalidating the word of God by your tradition which you have handed down; and you do many things such as that." The religious leaders prided themselves on their commitment to the Scriptures. They memorized large portions of the biblical text and debated its finer points of theology. Nonetheless, their vision was distorted because they viewed everything through the lens of religious tradition. As a result, they remained blind to the Bible's most basic truths (Matt. 15:14). As Jesus noted, the problem was far bigger than just the example of "corban." The religious leaders did many similar things. This was but one glaring symptom of a corrupt system in which tradition was given precedence over Scripture.

On the basis of their traditions, the Pharisees had accused Jesus's followers of being lawbreakers. In reality, the religious leaders were the real offenders. The Lord responded by condemning them based on the absolute standard of Scripture. He thereby established the principle that Scripture is authoritative over nonbiblical tradition. Then, as a confirmation of His verdict, Jesus pointed to appalling evidence of their hypocritical religion. The example He used demonstrated how absurd things can become (and how abusive a system can be) when tradition is allowed to supersede the Word of God.

REFORMATION COMPARISONS

Christ's rebuke of the Pharisees in Mark 7 serves as an important witness to the priority of Scripture over extrabiblical tradition. As noted at the beginning of this chapter, this was a central concern in the minds of the Protestant Reformers. When confronted with centuries of extrabiblical tradition, they insisted on obedience to the Word of God—even when doing so meant breaking away from certain traditional practices and teachings.

Like the first-century scribes and Pharisees, the leaders of the medieval Roman Catholic Church elevated extrabiblical traditions above the Word of God. To protect those traditions, they prohibited the translation of the Bible into the common languages of Europe. For example, in 1229 at the Synod of Toulouse, the church declared, "We prohibit that the laity should be permitted to have the books of the Old or New Testament."[3] The Council Tarragona in 1234 similarly stated, "No one may possess the books of the Old and New Testaments in the Romance [common] language, and if anyone possesses them he must turn them over to the local bishop within eight days after promulgation of this decree, so that they

[3] Cited from *Heresy and Authority in Medieval Europe*, ed. Edward Peters (Philadelphia: University of Pennsylvania Press, 1980), 195.

may be burned."[4] After John Wycliffe and his colleagues at Oxford finished their translation of the Bible into English, the Third Synod of Oxford (1408) condemned him for it, saying, "We therefore command and ordain that henceforth no one translate the text of Holy Scripture into English or any other language . . . . He who shall act otherwise let him be punished as an abettor of heresy and error."[5]

With medieval church services conducted in Latin, laypeople throughout Europe were kept in a perpetual state of spiritual darkness. They were purposely shielded from the Scriptures by a spiritually bankrupt system. The ignorance of the laity allowed the church to maintain its unbiblical traditions without being challenged by divine truth.

But, the Word of God could not be suppressed forever. The Lord raised up human instruments who recovered the study of biblical Hebrew and Greek. This enabled men like Martin Luther, William Tyndale, Miles Coverdale and others to translate the Scriptures from the original languages into the common languages of Europe. Even when Roman Catholic authorities banned such translation efforts, these faithful laborers understood that it is better to obey God than men. The printing press made it possible for copies of the Scripture to be printed en masse. As Bibles were disseminated, the Reformation became inevitable. When exposed to the light of God's truth, the shadowy traditions of medieval Roman Catholicism began to melt away. The Reformers expressed this reality using a Latin phrase, "*Post Tenebras Lux.*" It means, "After Darkness, Light." The dark grip of religious tradition gave way to the penetrating brilliance of biblical authority.

---

[4] Cited from Daniel Lortsch, *Historie de la Bible en France* (Société Biblique Britannique et Étrangère, 1910), 14.

[5] Cited from Thomas J. Carr, *The Church and the Bible* (Melbourne: Thomas E. Verga, 1895), 87.

IMPLICATIONS FOR TODAY

In Mark 7, Jesus elevated the authority of Scripture above that of tradition. That principle was at the center of the Protestant Reformation, as the truth of God's Word triumphed over the unbiblical traditions of the Roman Catholic Church. But what are the implications of this principle, both corporately and individually, for evangelical Christians today?

Corporately, Jesus's rebuke in Mark 7:6–9 provides a timely warning to the modern church. Though evangelicals generally are not enticed by either rabbinic customs or Roman Catholic traditions, the contemporary landscape is dotted with man-made authorities seeking to usurp the primacy of Scripture in the church. When felt needs take priority over clear biblical exposition, or market-driven strategies cloud out a biblical approach to ministry, or emotional ecstasy becomes a substitute for genuine worship, or scientific theories redefine the natural understanding of the biblical text—in such instances, the wisdom of man is being elevated above God's truth. Mark 7 serves as a vivid reminder that Scripture is authoritative over anything man-made. The call to the church is to stand unwaveringly upon the truth of God's Word. Jesus Christ is the Lord of the church. Accordingly, His Word is the supreme authority for the church. No matter how unpopular or outdated it may seem, believers must obey God rather than men.

On a personal level, the truth of Mark 7:1–13 challenges individual Christians to examine themselves, clearing away hypocrisy and bringing their conduct and speech into conformity with the Word of God. It is one thing to affirm the Reformation principle of *sola Scriptura*. It is altogether something else to practice that principle in everyday life—to long for the pure milk of the Word, to meditate on its riches, and to be doers of its truth and not hearers only.

The Reformation was the result of putting the authority of Christ and His Word back in its proper place, above the customs and ceremonies of medieval Roman Catholicism. In Mark 7, the

Lord Jesus established that very principle in His dialogue with the religious leaders of first-century Israel. Scripture's authority always supersedes that of tradition. When that order is reversed, the result inevitably displeases God and destroys people's lives. But when Scripture is elevated to its rightful position, God is honored as His people submit themselves to His perfect will.

In the sixteenth century, the church needed courageous leaders who were willing to defy man-made tradition in order to follow God's Word. That need still exists today. May the Lord raise up many who will boldly say, in the words of Peter, "We must obey God rather than men."

No.11

HEARING FROM HEAVEN:

How God Speaks Today (and How He Doesn't)

BY JUSTIN PETERS

"God said to me . . ." Undoubtedly you have heard those words, or something very similar. Ostensibly Christian television networks like TBN and Daystar are an endless parade of teachers claiming to hear from the Lord. The supposed prophets and apostles profess to hear God speak directly to them—either audibly, in some nebulous, "still small voice," or through dreams and visions. Some even claim Jesus appears to them physically to engage in conversation or impart some secret knowledge of present or future events. Moreover, countless shelves in Christian bookstores practically sag under the weight of books and DVDs promising to teach you how to more effectively hear and discern the voice of God.

The belief that God speaks to people in a direct, quotable sense outside of Scripture goes almost entirely uncontested in most evangelical circles today. To suggest otherwise is certain to garner plenty of bewildered looks and raised eyebrows. In fact, the vast majority of the evangelical world is often quick to dismiss anyone who questions the prevailing perspective on this issue as unspiritual and stodgy—they're seen as having exchanged a vibrant, loving relationship with Christ for cold, lifeless doctrine. But there's nothing inherently loving about undermining the truth of Scripture in favor of some private, personal word from the Lord. As we will see, such mystical pursuits are an implicit rejection of the authority and sufficiency of God's Word. God has spoken ultimately and finally in His Word, the sixty-six books of the Bible, and is not speaking today in any sense outside of Scripture. Making that case means first considering who is arguing for ongoing revelation from God, and how they defend their position.

HEARING VOICES

One of the modern charismatic movement's most prominent features is its enthusiastic acceptance and promotion of the belief that God still speaks today in dreams, visions, impressions, hunches, signs and wonders, and even through an audible voice. Wide—*very wide*—is the spectrum of popular charismatic preachers who claim that God speaks outside of the Bible. There are false teachers from the Word-Faith movement and the New Apostolic Reformation[1], such as Benny Hinn, Kenneth Copeland, Creflo Dollar, Jesse Duplantis, Todd White, Bill Johnson, and Todd Bentley—all who claim to hear personally from the Lord. Then there are the heretics and charlatans so brazen and outrageous that not even TBN or Daystar will carry their programs (which is saying something), such as Peter Popoff, Manasseh Jordan, and Robert Tilton. And there are more mainstream prosperity preachers, like Joel Osteen, Joseph Prince, Robert Morris, and Joyce Meyer.

Other popular preachers are difficult to label. Beth Moore and Priscilla Shirer, for example, do not teach classic Word-Faith

---

[1] For a more comprehensive critique of the Word-Faith and New Apostolic Reformation movements, see *Strange Fire* by Dr. John MacArthur and *Clouds Without Water II* by Justin Peters.

or prosperity theology per se, but they do associate and partner with many in those movements, and have adopted elements of their teaching, including our subject matter here. In addition, there are still others who would not subscribe to the heresy and chicanery of some of those listed above, but would still affirm that God can and does speak outside of the Bible today. Pastors and theologians like Wayne Grudem, Sam Storms, and Matt Chandler fall into this category. Though I differ with them in their charismatic position, I should stress that they would not affirm the likes of Benny Hinn, Kenneth Copeland, or Bill Johnson.

However, it is not just charismatics who believe God is still speaking outside of Scripture. I believe the book *Experiencing God*[2] by Henry Blackaby has done more to introduce charismatic theology into non-charismatic circles than any other single resource. Before *Experiencing God* was first published in 1990, most non-charismatics would have understood that we speak to God in prayer and God speaks to us in the Bible. But what used to be the norm is now the exception. Blackaby writes, "If you have trouble hearing God speak, you are in trouble at the very heart of your Christian experience."[3] Though many books offer instructions regarding how to hear God's voice, Blackaby says that the ability is derived not from a method, but that it "comes from an intimate love relationship with God."[4] In an interview with Joyce Meyer, Priscilla Shirer recalled a conversation she had with Blackaby: "Henry Blackaby said something to me one time; I was asking him about hearing the voice of God. . . . He said, 'Priscilla, you know, it's really simple. The more you know God, the more clearly you

---

[2] According to Henry Blackaby's official website, *Experiencing God* "has now been published in 47 languages and has been used in almost every denomination." Source: www.blackaby.org/experiencing-god/

[3] Henry T. Blackaby and Claude V. King, *Experiencing God* (Nashville: Broadman & Holman Publishers, 1994), 87.

[4] Ibid.

can hear Him.' . . . And I thought, How true that is!"[5]

Rick Warren, pastor of Saddleback Church in Lake Forest, CA, similarly teaches that believers *need* to hear from God.

> Last week we began a new miniseries on understanding how to hear the voice of God. Very few things are more important than this because you can't have a relationship to God if you can't hear God. If all you do is ever talk to Him in prayer, and you never hear God speak to you, that's a one-way relationship. That isn't much of a relationship. God wants to speak to you.[6]

Robert Morris, pastor of Gateway Church in Southlake, TX, likewise stresses the importance of relational intimacy with Christ.

> What is the main difference between a believer in Jesus Christ and a nonbeliever? What's the main difference? And let me give you the answer: It is that a believer has a personal relationship with Jesus Christ. . . . It's hard for me to believe that that personal relationship does not include communication. And yet there are entire persuasions of theological thought that God doesn't speak anymore. And that, to me, is crazy to think that way. That He spoke for four thousand years, and we have a record of Him speaking to person after person after person in the Old Testament and the New Testament, and then, all of a sudden, after the first century, He just got laryngitis, or He's just bursting up there because He hasn't talked to humans in over nineteen hundred years—it's just crazy to think that way. . . . But if you have a thought that God doesn't speak anymore . . . I feel so sorry for you—that you have a personal relationship

[5] Priscilla Shirer, "Know Your God," interview by Joyce Meyer, *Enjoying Everyday Life*, November 10, 2014, http://www.youtube.com/watch?v=gJc7Mc1ErYc.

[6] Rick Warren, "Learn How to Recognize God's Voice," sermon, Saddleback Church, October 7, 2014, Lake Forest, CA, Youtube video, https://www.youtube.com/watch?v=-827QmRDjUA.

with someone who never speaks to you. I don't know how personal that is.[7]

That desire to hear from God personally, outside the pages of His written Word, pervades the church today. Sarah Young is a name many Christian readers are familiar with—in the last fifteen years, she has become a juggernaut in the world of Christian publishing. Her devotional book *Jesus Calling* has sold tens of millions of copies, has been translated into twenty-six languages,[8] and has spawned numerous spinoff books.[9] Young's writing is the product of her desire to hear more from the Lord, coupled with her apparent dissatisfaction with what He has already said. In the introduction to *Jesus Calling*, she explains, "I knew that God communicated with me through the Bible, but I yearned for more."[10] The idea for the book came after Young read *God Calling*, a book by two anonymous "listeners" from the 1930s who, upon learning to tune in to God's "frequency," began to hear Him speak. They recorded the daily messages they received from Him with "pencils and paper in hand." These two listeners "felt . . . unworthy and overwhelmed by the wonder of it" and pitied the "millions of souls . . . [who] had to be content with guidance from the Bible."[11] Following that example, Young says, "I decided to listen to God with pen in hand

---

[7] Robert Morris, "I'm a Sheep," sermon, Gateway Church, April 16, 2016, Southlake, TX, Youtube video, https://www.youtube.com/watch?v=A6VQFe8s76Q

[8] Mark Oppenheimer, "A First-Person Defense of Writing in Jesus' Voice," *The New York Times*, October 25, 2013, Beliefs, https://www.nytimes.com/2013/10/26/us/from-sarah-young-the-author-of-jesus-calling-a-first-person-defense.html.

[9] Spin-offs include *Jesus Calling for Graduates, Dear Jesus, Jesus Lives, Jesus Calling for Encouragement, Jesus Always,* and *Jesus Today*. Source: https://www.jesuscalling.com/books/.

[10] Sarah Young, *Jesus Calling* (Nashville: Thomas Nelson, 2004), xii.

[11] "The Voice Divine," Two Listeners, accessed November 2018, https://www.twolisteners.org/ ?page_id=63.

writing down whatever I believed He was saying."[12]

The resulting devotionals are written in the first person, as though Christ Himself were speaking directly to the reader. And while Young attempts to differentiate her books from Scripture—saying, "I knew these writings were not as inspired as Scripture is, but they were helping me grow closer to God"[13]—she still intimates that they are somewhat inspired, and that her readers should likewise set aside their Bibles and attempt to hear privately and directly from God.

Dr. Charles Stanley[14] is another evangelical leader who routinely teaches that God speaks to him outside of Scripture. Once, a viewer of his program named Sally wrote to him and lamented,

> I have prayed for God to speak to me, but I don't hear Him. My faith is strong . . . but I have never heard Him say, "Go buy this gallon of milk, don't buy this car, wait for what I have for you." Am I not listening in the right way? Or is He guiding my everyday decisions, but I don't realized He's speaking? How do I hear God's voice?

Rather than assuring Sally that God has spoken to her in His sufficient Word and is not telling people where to buy milk and cars, Stanley replied,

> Speaking about buying groceries, on a particular day I had a very short period of time, and so I wanted to buy a turkey for Thanksgiving. My time was really running out. . . . I said, "God, just show me what to do." It's like God said, "Go to this store, buy the turkey now." Against sort of my will, I went. I

[12] Young, xiii.

[13] Ibid., xi, xii.

[14] Stanley is pastor of First Baptist Church, Atlanta, Georgia, and the former president of the Southern Baptist Convention (1984–1986).

> walked right in, straight to the right place, the right pound of turkey, walked right up, paid [for] it, got back in the car—in less than about twenty-five minutes. Did God tell me to go? Yes, He did.[15]

Stanley went on to say that God redirected him from buying one particular car by asking him, "Do you want this car, or do you want My best?" Stanley proceeded to tell the car salesman he was no longer interested and, presumably, bought another car that was God's "best."

This is nothing more than a modern version of Gnosticism.[16] Derived from the Greek word for "knowledge" (*gnōsis*), the ancient heresy of Gnosticism was based on a dualistic worldview that saw a sharp contrast between the physical and spiritual realms, and claimed that one could achieve true salvation only by gaining a secret, spiritual revelation. To receive that divine knowledge, one had to disengage all forms of rational thought. Today, many charismatics recommend a similar kind of mental disengagement if you want to hear from God.

But this is a false premise. The Bible never invites us to disengage our minds when it comes to the things of God. Upon being asked by a Pharisee what the greatest commandment was, Jesus responded, "You shall love the Lord your God with all your heart, with all your soul, and *with all your mind*" (Matt. 22:37, emphasis added). The apostle Paul instructed Timothy to "study to shew thyself approved unto God" (2 Tim. 2:15, KJV). God gave us a mind for a reason: He wants us to use it.

Additionally, let us dispense with the erroneous notion that knowledge of God and love for Him are somehow antithetical. Paul

---

[15] Charles Stanley, "How can I hear God's voice?," March 23, 2012, in *Ask Dr. Stanley*, produced by In Touch Ministries, Youtube video, https://www.youtube.com/watch?v=V4ocm31RJ7g.

[16] Likely allusions to (and rebuttals of) Gnosticism can be found in 1 Corinthians 15:44, 53; 1 Timothy 3:16, 6:20; and 2 John 7.

writes in Philippians 1:9, "This I pray, that your love may abound still more and more in real knowledge and all discernment." It is sound doctrine and right theology that deepen our knowledge of, and resultant love for, God. To put it another way, our love for Him can go only as deep as our knowledge of Him. The Bible never separates knowledge of God and love for Him; it always refers to them working in concert. And we know God by knowing His Word.

Consider the message these popular teachers send to the untold millions of people who trust them. It is that God speaks to these leaders on a regular basis—so much so that He tells them *where to buy groceries*—and that that should be the normative experience for every believer. But it is not. There are countless people like Sally who grow disheartened by God's silence and wonder why they're not in direct communication with Him like so many others supposedly are. It leads some to wonder if they are even saved. Perhaps you have wondered the same thing.

If you have wrestled with such questions, take heart. The Body of Christ is not divided into Haves and Have Nots—there aren't some Christians who get a direct line to God through dreams, visions, and audible voices, while the rest of us have to make do with *only* the Bible and the Holy Spirit. Scripture is clear: There is "one Lord, one faith, one baptism" (Eph. 4:5). All believers are indwelt by the same Holy Spirit (John 14:17; 1 Cor. 6:19–20) and enjoy the same intimate access to the same God (Heb. 4:16) through the same Savior (1 Tim. 2:5)—and "are all one in Christ Jesus" (Gal. 3:28). Untold numbers of God's people have wrestled with unnecessary doubts about their love for God, their knowledge of His Word, their spiritual maturity, even their very salvation, because of this egregious, unbiblical teaching.

PICKING APART THE PROOF TEXTS

Those who insist that God still speaks outside of Scripture believe their view is thoroughly biblical, and routinely employ several familiar texts in their defense. Let us consider a few of the more prominent ones.

And after the earthquake a fire; but the Lord was not in the fire: and after the fire a still small voice. (1 Kings 19:12, KJV)

The so-called "still small voice" of God is perhaps the primary means through which many people claim to hear from Him today. The phrase, borrowed from an episode in the life of the Old Testament prophet Elijah, is often applied to the way God supposedly speaks to believers through inward hunches or mental impressions. Many leaders in the church today urge Christians to listen to the voice of God inside them; the following tweet from Beth Moore is just one example: "There's a time to give up [and] a time to keep trying. Sometimes the time to keep trying feels a whole lot like time to give up. The only difference is the still small voice of the Holy Spirit within you saying, 'try again.'"[17]

Elijah bursts onto the scene in 1 Kings 17 by proclaiming God's judgment on Israel in the form of a devastating drought. In chapter 18, he dramatically defeated the prophets of Baal on Mount Carmel. After such a thunderous introduction, however, he flees from the wicked queen Jezebel (19:1–3), afraid for his life. Elijah fell into despair, inviting the Lord to take his life (v. 4). But the "angel of the Lord" delivered provisions (vv. 6–7) that would sustain Elijah on the long journey to a cave in Horeb, or Mount Sinai (v. 8). There he encountered powerful manifestations of God's power and presence: a strong wind, an earthquake, and fire (vv. 11–12). But Scripture makes a point to tell us repeatedly that the Lord was not in them. Instead, verse 12 tells us that after the fire, Elijah heard "a sound of a gentle blowing" (the ESV translates it as "the sound of a low whisper"). The King James Bible translates the Hebrew as "a still small voice," or what we could call in literal terms, "a voice of sheer quiet." Elijah heard *something*—something *quiet*. But it was coming from outside of the cave, and he could not tell what it was.

[17] Beth Moore (@BethMooreLPM), Twitter, July 2, 2018, 5:47 a.m., https://twitter.com/bethmoorelpm/status/1013765999143849985.

Upon hearing it, Elijah "wrapped his face in his mantle and went out and stood in the entrance of the cave. And behold, a voice came to him and said, 'What are you doing here, Elijah?'" (v. 13).

At no point in Elijah's story are we instructed to follow his example. This is not a pattern or a prescription for hearing directly from God. We must not fail to recognize this as a specific and unique instance, even in the life of the prophet who regularly heard from God. This wasn't routine in the Old Testament, and we should not imagine that it is today either. Moreover, the voice Elijah heard was not some mere mental impression. It was external to him. It was not "within" Elijah, as Beth Moore and nearly every other teacher who cites this text suggest. Elijah walked out of the cave, and Yahweh spoke to him audibly and unmistakably.

My sheep hear My voice, and I know them, and they follow Me. (John 10:27)

When it comes to people claiming to hear from God, there is little doubt that John 10:27 is the most widely used and abused verse. I have seen countless evangelical leaders cite this verse as proof that God speaks to His sheep outside of the Bible. It is the primary proof text for defending extrabiblical revelation. In his book *Frequency: Tune In, Hear God*, Robert Morris says, "So the teaching in John 10 is clear. Who is Jesus? Jesus is our Good Shepherd. And what are we? We're sheep. And how does the Good Shepherd guide His sheep? By His voice. That's how we're to live: by listening to Jesus' voice. We're to depend on hearing His voice regularly and clearly."[18]

Morris is right when he points out that John 10:27 teaches that Jesus is the Good Shepherd and believers are His sheep. But he is quite wrong when he then says that the verse is about us hearing God's voice *outside* of Scripture once we learn to tune in to His "frequency." One need only read the passage in its context

---

[18] Robert Morris, *Frequency: Tune In, Hear God* (Nashville: W Publishing Group, 2016), 9.

to grasp the clear meaning of Christ's words. The voice of the Shepherd is calling His sheep to salvation. The entire chapter deals with Jesus calling His "own sheep by name" (v. 3), and that they "will be saved, and will go in and out and find pasture" (v. 9). After Jesus says, "My sheep hear My voice" in verse 27, He immediately follows with a statement that makes His point unequivocally clear: "I give eternal life to them, and they will never perish; and no one will snatch them out of My hand" (v. 28).

The Shepherd's voice in John 10 is the effectual calling of His sheep to repentance and faith. This is the voice of the Lord calling us to eternal life, not telling us where to buy our Thanksgiving turkey. Pretending otherwise trivializes the beautiful illustration of Christ's love for His people.

Jesus Christ is the same yesterday and today and forever. (Heb. 13:8)

This verse has nothing to do with God speaking to His people; nonetheless, those who believe in ongoing revelation often cite it. They attempt to use God's immutability—the doctrinal term for His unchanging nature, character, and attributes—to make the case that God always functions and operates in the same way. The argument is that the Lord spoke to numerous people in both the Old and New Testaments, and because He does not change, He must be doing so today, as well. This same verse is also deployed to argue for modern-day apostles and miracle workers.

The constant abuse and misuse of this verse comes down to faulty logic. It confuses the *descriptive* with the *prescriptive*, as we discussed in looking at 1 Kings 19. In other words, not everything that is described in the Bible is prescribed for believers—every event the Bible records is a historic reality and did occur, but that doesn't mean it is normative for today. Plenty of the miracles recorded in Scripture were one-time events. God made an ax head float for Elisha (2 Kings 6). In Numbers 22, He spoke through a donkey. Is He any less God because those miracles are not continuously occurring today?

In fact, it is worth pointing out that even though God did audibly speak to numerous people across the Old and New Testaments, He was not speaking as often as most people seem to think. Some well-known biblical figures, such as Hezekiah, Ezra, Nehemiah, and Esther, never heard the audible voice of God. And there was a period of four hundred years between the Old and New Testaments when God didn't say anything to anyone. Moreover, when God *did* speak, people knew exactly what He said. That includes men who were unregenerate at the time God spoke to them: Saul (Acts 9) recognized the voice of his Creator. He did not have an intimate relationship with the Lord when He spoke to him—he was actively trying to eradicate Christianity!—yet he knew it was He.

The subjectivity, ambiguity, and individuality with which God supposedly speaks today is a modern construct without any biblical support or precedent.

HOW GOD SPEAKS

To understand how God *does speak* today, let us go to what He has said already in Scripture. "God, after He spoke long ago to the fathers in the prophets in many portions and in many ways, in these last days has spoken to us in His Son, whom He appointed heir of all things, through whom also He made the world" (Heb. 1:1–2).

The anonymous author of Hebrews wastes no time, diving directly into the deep end of the theological pool. The entire thrust of the epistle is to establish and extoll the superiority of Christ over the Old Testament and the old covenant between God and Israel. Christ offers a better hope and a better covenant for His people. He is our better High Priest, offering a better sacrifice, and securing for us a better reward. In keeping with that theme, the author tells us in these opening verses that Jesus is the better and fullest messenger from God.

The writer affirms that God is a relational God—that is, He speaks to His people. He's not the god of deism, who created and immediately withdrew from creation. The Creator God of the Bible is not distant; He condescends and relates to His people. He speaks to them. Looking back through history, the writer of Hebrews explains that God had spoken to His covenant people in the Old Testament "in many portions and in many ways." God spoke to Moses through a burning bush (Ex. 3) and through thunder, lightning, and fire on Sinai (Ex. 19). He spoke through a dream to Jacob (Gen. 31), and through visions to Abraham (Gen. 15) and Isaiah (Isa. 6). As we already noted, He even spoke to Balaam through a donkey (Num. 22).

But as magnificent as God's multitudinous acts of speaking were, they were only partial. All of them looked forward to the ultimate fulfillment of God's redemptive plan. The Old Testament prophets had only bits and pieces of a much larger picture—one that came into crystal-clear focus in God's Son, Jesus Christ. And God required His prophets to get the message right. God said to Moses, "I will raise up a prophet . . . and I will put My words in his mouth, and he shall speak to them all that I command him" (Deut. 18:18). The standard for Old Testament prophets was perfection, not in personal conduct, but in accurately communicating God's words (Deut. 13:2–3; 18:22; Jer. 23:31–32). The punishment for a prophetic failure was death (Deut. 18:20). Scripture is clear that it is a presumptuous blasphemy to say God said something that He never said. Moreover, it's clear God takes such outrageous sin seriously. Consider these condemning words He delivered through the prophet Jeremiah:

> Do not listen to the words of the prophets who are prophesying to you. They are leading you into futility; they speak a vision of their own imagination, not from the mouth of the Lord. (23:16)

> I did not send these prophets, but they ran. I did not speak to them, but they prophesied. (23:21)

> I have heard what the prophets have said who prophesy falsely in My name, saying, "I had a dream, I had a dream!" (23:25)

> "Behold, I am against those who have prophesied false dreams," declares the Lord, "and related them and led My people astray by their falsehoods and reckless boasting; yet I did not send them or command them, nor do they furnish this people the slightest benefit," declares the Lord. (23:32)

When it comes to those who pretend to speak on His behalf, God does not mince words. He does not take lightly those who put their own words into His mouth. It is a woeful blasphemy—one that God explicitly says does not furnish anyone the slightest benefit.

Some today, though, are attempting to argue that New Testament prophecy has somehow been redefined, and modern "prophets" should not be held to the same standard as their Old Testament counterparts. Modern prophecy, they say, can be fallible. Sam Storms is a charismatic pastor and theologian. Regarding messages that might be from God, he says we should "introduce prophetic utterances with statements such as: 'I have a strong inner impression that I believe is from the Lord' [and] 'I have a picture in my mind that I think may be for someone here.'"[19] But the language and the caveats he recommends are foreign to Scripture. Can you imagine Moses or Isaiah saying, "I have a strong inner impression and a picture in my mind that I think possibly might be from God for you"? Ridiculous! Rather, we consistently see true prophets boldly declaring, "The word of the Lord came to me" (Jer. 1:4; Ezek. 12:1). "The word of the Lord came" to Hosea (1:1), Joel (1:1), Micah (1:1), Zephaniah (1:1), Haggai (1:1), and Zechariah (1:1). John heard "a loud voice like the sound of a trumpet" (Rev. 1:10). It doesn't seem God had any trouble speaking clearly to His prophets in the Old and New Testaments.

Storms is far from alone in accepting fallible messages from an infallible God. Matt Chandler—pastor of a Southern Baptist megachurch in the Dallas area—seems even less concerned with the

---

[19] Sam Storms, *Practicing the Power* (Grand Rapids, MI: Zondervan, 2017), 129.

danger presented by supposed words from the Lord that did not come from Him.

> One of the ways that God speaks is through pictures, that may or may not make sense to us, but be insight into another person in a way that they feel seen, known, loved, and built up. Now, because we're Bible people, . . . this stuff's scary. . . . Let's have some real talk real quick: What if we're only talking to ourselves? What if we're like, "OK, Lord, will you show me somebody that I might encourage? . . ." and somebody pop in our head, [but] that's just us? OK, look at me. You got me? *So what?* Oh no—you're going to encourage somebody! Right? Like why would that be this terrible thing?[20]

To answer his rhetorical question, yes, it is a terrible thing because it's *not true*. There is no validity in ascribing to God the ideas and internal inclinations that are more likely the products of your imagination, or of the pizza you ate last night. Any doubts about their origin ought to be enough to keep us from crediting internal impressions to God. Those who have been redeemed through the sacrifice of His Son and have been renewed through the work of His Spirit ought to have more respect for His Word than that. God's people ought to take Him seriously—seriously enough not to be dismissive about whether He is speaking to them. Christians must not be so cavalier about mistaking their own imaginations for the voice of God.

In his sermon, Chandler stated that the prophesying of which he spoke does not rise to the same level as the prophecy of Scripture. But such a distinction is completely arbitrary and artificial. The Bible makes no such distinction, and the book of Hebrews puts an end to such vanity. As the author explains, God once spoke to His people

[20] Matt Chandler, "A Supernatural Community and A Personal Word," sermon, The Village Church, July 16, 2018, Flower Mound, TX, Youtube video, https://www.youtube.com/watch?v=n0aB1lolHn0.

"in many portions and in many ways" (1:1), but His Word has been ultimately fulfilled and revealed in Jesus Christ. He "has spoken to us in His Son" (v. 2) fully and completely, like never before. This declaration could not be more opposite the murky impressions accepted today as divine revelation.

What more needs to be said? Under the guidance of the Holy Spirit, the apostle Paul wrote these conclusive words: "All Scripture is inspired by God and profitable for teaching, for reproof, for correction, for training in righteousness; so that the man of God may be adequate, equipped for every good work" (2 Tim. 3:16–17). Those verses stand as a towering testament against those who would say the Bible is not enough. Within the closed canon is everything we need to live a life of faithful obedience to God and, in doing so, glorify Him.

The Holy Spirit knew that it would not be long before men and women would come and claim new dreams and new visions and new revelations from God, thereby attempting to add to His words. Mohammed's new revelation gave us Islam. Joseph Smith's new revelation gave us Mormonism. Mary Baker Eddy's new revelation gave us Christian Science. Men strayed from Scripture's sufficiency, intermingled pagan idolatry, redefined grace, created an unbiblical hierarchical structure, kept the Bible out of the hands of men and women, and gave us Roman Catholicism. Practically every apostate religion and cult after the apostolic age has begun with a man or woman saying, "God has spoken to me; let me tell you what He had to say."

Everything God has to say to us, He has said in His Son Jesus Christ, and we have a full, inerrant, infallible, all-sufficient record of that in the completed canon. When the Bible speaks, God speaks. There is nothing that can or should be added to what is already perfect, settled, and sealed in the pages of God's Word. To presume to add to what is already the perfect Word of God is to presume to add to His perfect Son.

THE ALL-SUFFICIENT WORD

It has always been the duty of God's people to defend the truth of His Word. Decades ago, the primary battlefront was the inerrancy of Scripture: in the 1970s largely within the Lutheran Church—Missouri Synod, and in the 1980s within the Southern Baptist Convention. In many ways, those battles were won, protecting biblical inerrancy and establishing it as a foundational evangelical doctrine. And while those fires still smolder in some corners of evangelicalism, the real battle today, I would argue, is over the *sufficiency* of Scripture. It is a battle we are losing rapidly and dramatically. The belief that God speaks outside of Scripture is an overt denial of its sufficiency.

God's people are not to seek after signs (Matt. 16:4) and are to guard against being taken "captive through philosophy and empty deception" (Col. 2:8). Instead we are to "let the word of Christ dwell richly within" us (Col. 3:16), and hold fast to sound doctrine and refute those who contradict the same (Titus 1:9). Some say that a closed canon results in a cold, boring, and even lifeless version of Christianity devoid of emotion. Nothing could be further from the truth! God says in Jeremiah 23:29, "Is not My word like fire . . . and like a hammer which shatters a rock?" Does that sound boring and lifeless to you? His Word is alive. It is "living and active" (Heb. 4:12), and is the Holy Spirit's means of renewing our minds (Rom. 12:2) and conforming us to the image of Christ (Rom. 8:29) as He indwells and helps believers, through diligent and careful study, to understand God's Word. He illuminates the meaning of Scripture to our minds and empowers us to obey it to the glory of God. How can this not deeply stir our emotions and thrill our hearts? For the true child of God, it does.

Furthermore, for all of the trees cut down and the ink spilt to give us the mountain of books on how to hear God's voice, it's amazing that God's book has no such instructions. One would think that if this were such an integral part of the Christian experience, the Bible would be full of instructions, tips, or *something* to help us hear from God more clearly and accurately. But it isn't. In fact, in all the letters Paul wrote to new and often struggling churches, he gave plenty of instruction relating to church polity, qualifications for leaders, holding fast to sound doctrine, defending against false teachers, and holy living in general. But nowhere will you find him giving instructions on how to hear God's voice. Peter doesn't address it either. Neither do James or John. In fact, not even Jesus Himself gives us any pointers. If learning to hear God's voice outside of Scripture is so vitally important for the church in the post-apostolic age, one would think God would have instructed us how to do it.

God used to speak in many portions and in many ways, but He now speaks to us in His all-sufficient Word. If you want to hear God speak to you, read your Bible. If you want to hear God speak audibly, read it out loud!

John MacArthur has championed the sufficiency of Scripture over more than half a century of preaching and teaching. It has been one of the hallmarks of his faithful ministry. He has modeled for me and so many others how to boldly and unapologetically speak the Bible's unvarnished truth, and yet do so with love and grace. May we follow his example, as he follows Christ.

I'll close with the words of a treasured hymn that celebrates the quality and character of God's Word.

> How firm a foundation, ye saints of the Lord,
> Is laid for your faith in His excellent Word!
> What more can He say than to you He hath said—
> To you who for refuge to Jesus have fled?

What more can He say to us, dear ones, than what He has already said in His Word?

No.12

THE FOOLISHNESS OF THE CROSS

BY PHIL JOHNSON

One of the most startling and instructive passages the apostle Paul ever wrote comes in the opening three chapters of 1 Corinthians. It is an extended discussion of wisdom versus foolishness. That would of course be a standard topic for practically every rabbi, philosopher, poet, or spiritual mentor. But the apostle deliberately turns the conventional vocabulary and values all upside down. He categorically abhors human wisdom, and he speaks of "the foolishness of God" in glowing terms. He disparages might, nobility, and intellectual prowess while exalting "the foolish ... the weak ... and the base things of the world"—oh, and "the despised" as well (1 Cor. 1:27–28).

This is the man once known as Saul of Tarsus, a descendant of Pharisees who (at a remarkably young age) had become a high-ranking Pharisee himself. He seemed better equipped than anyone else in his generation to rise to the top of the Sanhedrin, Judaism's ruling council. In effect, they were the spiritual illuminati of that time and culture, and to gain prominence in their midst was no small accomplishment. But even as a young man, Saul could stand shoulder to shoulder with the most noble and most knowledgeable of them. He was a true scholar, trained from childhood in Jerusalem, on the Temple mount, among the Sanhedrin, at the feet of Gamaliel, the leading scholar and most influential rabbi of the first century. Paul's head was full of knowledge about Jewish tradition and the Hebrew Scriptures. He was also well-versed in both logic and literature from a wide-ranging background—able to quote verbatim from ancient Greek philosophers and poets. He was as skilled in legal matters as any lawyer. Most of all, he was an expert in all things pertaining to Jewish ceremonial religion.

We would perhaps expect someone with such a background to exalt the earthly symbols of good breeding and refinement: wisdom, grandeur, high culture, artistry, academic achievement, scholarship, sophistication, social status, stylishness, elegance, popularity, power, prestige, and other similar traits typically held in high esteem by religious people. But after Paul's conversion, he regarded all such human achievements as utterly worthless—of no more value than dung.

Literally the *only* realities Paul treasured were found in Christ, beginning with the surpassing value of knowing Him, "and the power of His resurrection and the fellowship of His sufferings, being conformed to His death; in order [to] attain to the resurrection from the dead" (Phil. 3:10–11). Of course, he also cherished the fellowship of other believers, practically none of whom had any esteem in the eyes of the world. Paul knew this was by God's sovereign design. God did not choose and redeem people because of any merit He saw in them. To those Corinthian Christians who were jockeying for celebrity status or contending with one another for power and prestige, Paul made this point with blunt candor:

> Consider your calling, brethren, that there were not many wise according to the flesh, not many mighty, not many noble; but God has chosen the foolish things of the world to shame the

> wise, and God has chosen the weak things of the world to shame the things which are strong, and the base things of the world and the despised God has chosen, the things that are not, so that He may nullify the things that are, so that no man may boast before God. (1 Cor. 1:26–29)

It's intriguing that this is practically the starting point of 1 Corinthians, because the church in Corinth was notoriously struggling with a vast catalog of serious problems. There was strife and division in the church. Meanwhile, they were ignoring serious immorality in their midst. Their corporate gatherings were grossly out of control with drunkenness, gluttony, and foolish competition over their individual spiritual gifts. They were literally vying with one another to see who could claim the most important or most spectacular charismatic gifting. There was so much confusion over vital tenets of the faith that the church was in imminent danger of falling into serious heresy. (Paul's long discourse in chapter 15 suggests that someone in Corinth was even denying the bodily resurrection of Christ.) Women were challenging the authority of their husbands. Church members were suing one another in secular courts.

In short, this was a twenty-first-century-style church, and Paul wrote this epistle to deal with that baffling assortment of very serious problems, one by one. The average church planter might have simply given up in despair, closed the church, and written the Corinthian assembly off as a nest of false converts. Not Paul. He poured his life into his people. The Corinthians seem not to have appreciated that about Paul, but it's the very thing that made his ministry so effective.

It's significant that, given all those shocking problems, the first one Paul singles out and responds to is the strife caused by the culture of celebrity that had developed in that church: "There are quarrels among you. Now I mean this, that each one of you is saying, 'I am of Paul,' and 'I of Apollos,' and 'I of Cephas,' and 'I of Christ'" (1 Cor. 1:11–12). He opens the epistle with more than three chapters on that one issue alone, rebuking the Corinthian church members repeatedly for the arrogance underlying their boasting, their rivalries, their craving for human applause, their struggle for status in the eyes of men, and the careless way they had imbibed the values and fashions of the world around them.

The petty rivalries Paul describes might at first glance seem to be the least of the Corinthians' problems. When you have a church member fornicating with his father's wife, a gross and shocking sin like that would normally be treated as a more pressing problem than silly arguments between home-study groups that are at odds with one another over which author or theologian is their favorite teacher to follow.

But this was Paul's starting point—and an issue he spent multiple chapters dealing with—because it highlighted the fundamental error underlying every one of the other difficulties that church was struggling with. Namely, *they were seeking favor from men, rather than striving to please God.* They were obsessed with gaining esteem and approval from others. They were too concerned with what was fashionable or impressive in the assessment of their neighbors.

It was why they took a lax attitude toward sin in their midst. Some regarded their tolerance of a gross fornicator as a badge of sophistication—a reason to boast (5:2). It's also why they were wobbly on the resurrection. After all, nothing was more unfashionable in Greek intellectual society than the idea of bodily resurrection. No doubt some in the church were fearful that if they didn't adjust and contextualize, or at least tone down, that aspect of the Christian faith, they could never enjoy esteem among the Greek intelligentsia.

In short, the Corinthian church was a hotbed of first-century hipster religion.

Careful readers will also notice that Paul's answer to every one of the Corinthian assembly's problems ultimately pointed them back to the gospel. In fact, he started the whole epistle with a reference to the gospel and the eternal benefits the Corinthians had derived from receiving it:

> I thank my God always concerning you for the grace of God which was given you in Christ Jesus, that in everything you were enriched in Him, in all speech and all knowledge, even as the testimony concerning Christ was confirmed in you, so that you are not lacking in any gift, awaiting eagerly the revelation of our Lord Jesus Christ, who will also confirm you to the end, blameless in the day of our Lord Jesus Christ. God is faithful, through whom you were called into fellowship with His Son, Jesus Christ our Lord. (1 Cor. 1:4–9)

That first chapter closes with a one-verse summary of the gospel, replete with a Calvinistic emphasis: "*By His doing* you are in Christ Jesus, who became to us wisdom from God, and righteousness and sanctification, and redemption" (v. 30, emphasis added).

Paul ends the epistle with the gospel, too. At the beginning of chapter 15, he gives a clear, simple summary of the historical facts of the gospel. That is the foundation on which he bases that long discussion showing why the bodily resurrection of Christ is the linchpin of gospel truth.

So the whole epistle keeps a steady focus on gospel truth throughout, and in chapter 1 Paul ties the gospel itself with the point he is making about divine foolishness and human wisdom:

> For the word of the cross is foolishness to those who are perishing, but to us who are being saved it is the power of God. For it is written,
>
> "I will destroy the wisdom of the wise,
> And the cleverness of the clever I will set aside."
>
> Where is the wise man? Where is the scribe? Where is the debater of this age? Has not God made foolish the wisdom of the world? For since in the wisdom of God the world through

> its wisdom did not come to know God, God was well-pleased through the foolishness of the message preached to save those who believe. For indeed Jews ask for signs and Greeks search for wisdom; but we preach Christ crucified, to Jews a stumbling block and to Gentiles foolishness, but to those who are the called, both Jews and Greeks, Christ the power of God and the wisdom of God. Because the foolishness of God is wiser than men, and the weakness of God is stronger than men.
>
> For consider your calling, brethren, that there were not many wise according to the flesh, not many mighty, not many noble; but God has chosen the foolish things of the world to shame the wise, and God has chosen the weak things of the world to shame the things which are strong, and the base things of the world and the despised God has chosen, the things that are not, so that He may nullify the things that are, so that no man may boast before God. (vv. 18–29)

I have always had a special fondness for that passage of Scripture, and no doubt it has had a major impact on my perspective of ministry because the Lord used that text and the truth Paul stresses in that section of Scripture to awaken me to the reality that I desperately needed to repent and trust Christ. My first reading of that passage began a sequence of events that quickly brought me to repentance and faith.

Furthermore, in nearly four decades of working with John MacArthur, I have been reminded of this passage repeatedly. It succinctly distills one of the most prominent themes in the philosophy of ministry that Pastor MacArthur has taught and modeled throughout his years in the pastorate. It is the chief biblical answer to the sinful pragmatism that dominates the evangelical movement today. And it is an ideal compass for anyone seeking a biblical perspective on how we as believers—and the church collectively—must seek to honor Christ in the eyes of a hostile world.

There's far too much in that passage to do a full exposition of the complete text in a single chapter, so what I want to do here is take a more focused look at verse 21 and consider some of its implications. That verse neatly summarizes the central point of the larger pericope, and it also clearly states what I personally would regard as the single, most distinctive element in the philosophy of ministry John MacArthur has inculcated into Grace Community Church, Grace to You, The Master's Seminary, and scores of men whom he has trained for ministry.

But first, permit me to give a brief testimony about the impact this section of 1 Corinthians had in my own conversion.

As a seventeen-year-old, one month away from high school graduation, I picked up a Bible one night and opened it at random, intending by chance to select and read just a verse or two as if it were a fortune-cookie message. In God's providence, my Bible fell open that night to the first page of 1 Corinthians, so that's where I began reading. Something drew me in further, and I kept going. By the time I got to chapter 3, I was deeply under conviction. What stood out most starkly to me was the absolute contempt God has for the wisdom of this world. It defied every expectation I had ever entertained about what it takes to have God's approval. I had always thought that if I studied the best of this world's wisdom, fought for the highest of moral and ethical principles, cultivated a working knowledge of the world's most brilliant philosophies, and fostered an appreciation for the finest expressions of art, music, and culture, God would surely be pleased with that. But in verse 19, Paul is quoting from Isaiah 29:14, where God Himself is speaking: "I will destroy the wisdom of the wise, and the cleverness of the clever I will set aside."

Paul goes on for chapters, and these statements seemed to leap out at me: "Your faith [should] not rest on the wisdom of men, but on the power of God" (2:5). "Let no man deceive himself. If any man among you thinks that he is wise in this age, he must become foolish, so that he may become wise. For the wisdom of this world is foolishness before God" (3:18–19).

It would have made perfect sense to me if God said He hated

the *foolish* things of this world. I already knew that He is too holy to approve what is vile and ignoble. But as I read these opening chapters of 1 Corinthians, it suddenly became very clear to me that the sins I was most ashamed of weren't even my biggest problem; my pride, my self-sufficiency, and the belief that I was good enough to merit God's favor were also evil. In fact, God says He hates the very things I thought were my *best* qualities—especially my infatuation with human wisdom. According to 1 Corinthians 3:18, if I really wanted to be wise, I needed to become a fool for Christ's sake.

Instantly, and for the first time in my life, I became keenly aware of how lost and sinful I truly was.

Over the next few days, God sovereignly orchestrated a series of unplanned and totally unexpected events that ultimately resulted in my hearing a sermon on the crucifixion. The preacher's text was Isaiah 53, and he explained the gospel clearly and unapologetically. That's how the way of salvation finally became totally clear to me. In other words, what brought me to Christ was the plain text of Scripture followed by clear, biblical preaching—minus any of the games and gimmicks the typical twenty-first-century evangelical thinks are essential to reach young people.

That is precisely how Paul says it should be: "For since in the wisdom of God the world through its wisdom did not come to know God, God was well-pleased through the foolishness of the message preached to save those who believe" (1 Cor. 1:21).

That, again, is the verse I want to unpack. It is not complex. "The message preached" is of course the gospel. Paul says in an earlier verse that Christ sent him "to preach the gospel, not in cleverness of speech" (v. 17). And the substance of the message is not about rehabilitating the culture, redeeming the arts, or reconstructing the world's political machinery. It is about the sacrifice Christ made for His people's sins. "We preach Christ crucified" (v. 23). Paul is emphatic about this: "When I came to you, brethren, I did not come with superiority of speech or of wisdom, proclaiming to you the testimony of God. For I determined to know nothing among you except Jesus Christ, and Him crucified" (2:1–2).

That message is the only effective answer to the evils of this present age. That is why the only strategy God has given to the church for reaching the lost is the simple, distinct, and accurate proclamation of the gospel. That is the gist of Paul's point in 1 Corinthians 1:21.

Virtually all the practical implications arising from that verse are diametrically opposed to the conventional wisdom we are accustomed to hearing from church-growth strategists nowadays. I particularly want to note three ideas conveyed in the text: *First*, Paul says emphatically that worldly wisdom does not save sinners. *Second*, he notes that the only message that can save sinners seems like sheer foolishness. And *third*, God is pleased when we don't festoon His "foolishness" with this world's wisdom.

Let's consider those points in order.

WORLDLY WISDOM

One phrase in the middle of the verse seemed to jump out at me the first time I read it: "The world through its wisdom did not come to know God." It is not possible to find God through the pursuit of worldly wisdom. Philosophy, politics, arts and aesthetics—and every other kind of worldly wisdom—is utterly devoid of power to transform a sinner into a saint. Only one thing can give a sinner a new heart, and that is spiritual regeneration—the new birth—by the agency of the Holy Spirit.

The instrument used by the Spirit to accomplish regeneration is the Word of God. According to 1 Peter 1:23, we are "born again not of seed which is perishable but imperishable, that is, through the living and enduring word of God." God's Word also has innate power to cleanse and sanctify. Jesus told His disciples in John 15:3, "You are already clean because of the word which I have spoken to you."

Only the Word of God, and specifically the gospel message, has the power to transform people's hearts and change them at the very core of who they are. The gospel "is the power of God for salvation to everyone who believes" (Rom. 1:16), and that is why the apostle Paul said, "I am not ashamed of the gospel"—even though the gospel seems foolish and naïve to those steeped in the wisdom of this world.

Educational programs, legislative policies, and political agendas can never turn sinners into good people. All those things are worldly wisdom, and they constitute a carnal and utterly ineffectual strategy for reforming any society that is in love with sin. In fact, if righteousness could be brought about by legislation, the gospel would be superfluous. Paul said that very thing in Galatians 2:21: "If righteousness comes through the Law, then Christ died needlessly." He said it again in Galatians 3:21: "If a law had been given which was able to impart life, then righteousness would indeed have [come by] law."

But neither society nor individuals can be redeemed by worldly wisdom. Christians are seriously deluded if they think the most important battles for righteousness are being waged in the arenas of politics, education, and the arts. Those are the realms of worldly wisdom—a wisdom that can never save.

Why? Because, according to Luke 10:21, God has "hidden these things from the wise and intelligent and . . . revealed them to infants. . . . For this way was well-pleasing in [His] sight." If saving truth were something to be found through worldly wisdom, then only the wise could be saved. But God has chosen to make the truth simple so even simple-minded folk can grasp it.

Furthermore, God forbids us to use fleshly weapons and worldly strategies to enforce moral standards on people. In Matthew 20:25–28, Jesus said, "You know that the rulers of the Gentiles lord it over them, and their great men exercise authority over them. It is not this way among you, but whoever wishes to become great among you shall be your servant, and whoever wishes to be first among you shall be your slave; just as the Son of Man did not come to be served, but to serve, and to give His life a ransom for many."

Worldly wisdom, political strategies, human cleverness, and the like cannot redeem either society or individuals. But there is one means by which God has chosen to make the maximum impact on sinful people. It's not a complex scheme, and it won't seem like a very shrewd master plan to anyone who is convinced that opinion polls, spreadsheets, cultural savvy, and the art of contextualization are necessary tools for effective church growth. Indeed, Paul acknowledges that God's chosen strategy will seem utterly inane to any carnal wisdom-seeker. He even refers to it as "the foolishness of God" (1 Cor. 1:25).

HEAVENLY FOOLISHNESS

Nevertheless, the apostle says, "God was well-pleased through the foolishness of the message preached to save those who believe." The Greek expression for "the message preached" is *kērygmatos* ("the proclamation"). It can be taken two ways. It might mean that although preaching seems a foolish strategy, it is the methodology God chose. That's how the King James Version renders the verse: "It pleased God by the foolishness of *preaching* to save them that believe"—referring to the unsophisticated means by which the gospel is delivered. It is more likely that Paul is using *kērygmatos* as a reference to the gospel itself. It is the message itself that seems most foolish, not merely the means by which it is disseminated.

Both context and idiom suggest that the "foolishness" Paul spoke of was not merely preaching as a strategy, but the actual content of the gospel message. "We preach Christ crucified . . . [even though] to Gentiles [it is] foolishness" (v. 23). Most modern translations are therefore correct to say, "the foolishness of the message preached."

Let's face it squarely, as Paul did: the gospel is a message that seems ineffectual and hopelessly naïve to the unregenerate mind. But this supposed foolishness is actually the wisdom of God, which is wiser than men. Therefore, the preaching of the gospel is the most potent weapon we could unleash against the sins of our society. It is the only thing that can give life to a spiritually dead heart—even though unregenerate people will invariably deem it absolute foolishness unless and until the Lord opens their hearts to receive it.

Again, Paul is directly arguing against the mindset that prevails in most contemporary evangelical circles. The mentality that has engineered so many massive yet spiritually impotent megachurches *starts* with opinion polls and surveys to see what people want. They canvass the neighborhood to find out people's tastes. They ask "unchurched" people what they want in a religious experience, and then they purposely adapt the message and the ministries to "meet the felt needs" of worldly people. By purely pragmatic standards, where the main goal is to attract an appreciative crowd, it works. Offer people what they are asking for, and they will come.

That is the dominant philosophy in most of the church planting being done today. Virtually all the monster-size megachurches follow that plan. It is the prevailing wisdom being taught in seminaries, church-growth seminars, and textbooks on ministry philosophy today. It's why churches tailor music, the atmosphere, and even their sermon topics to suit the tastes and preferences of the audience.

There's no question that the give-people-what-they-want approach can be effective in drawing huge crowds. It's the reason megachurch attendance has grown and churches embracing pragmatic philosophies have proliferated around the world over the past two decades. But can such a strategy be effective in the long-term? Has this approach truly stimulated genuine, faithful commitment to Christ? Does it promote sanctification? Are such churches known for spiritual depth? Do they encourage people to live consistently for Christ?

The answer to each of those questions is an unequivocal *no*. It is not a biblical strategy. It is precisely the thing Paul says not to do.

Don't miss the significance of verse 22: "Jews ask for signs and Greeks search for wisdom." If Paul followed the strategy recommended by modern church-growth experts, what would he do? Wouldn't he *give* the Jews signs and contextualize his preaching to Greeks by integrating the style and substance of their favorite philosophers?

That is of course the very approach many people today do advocate. Even some who insist they would never abandon the gospel nevertheless show an eager willingness to mold and shape the message so it sounds like wisdom to people who value philosophical sophistication.

But notice what the apostle Paul says: "We preach Christ crucified, to Jews a stumbling block and to Gentiles foolishness" (v. 23). Jewish people want a sign; we give them a stumbling-block. Greeks want wisdom; we give them foolishness.

Why? Was Paul just being obstinate or disagreeable? Of course not. He explains his rationale: "To those who are the called, both Jews and Greeks, Christ [is] the power of God and the wisdom of God" (v. 24). The gospel is the greatest sign of all, and it is the greatest wisdom of all "*to those who are the called.*" The elect see both power and wisdom in the gospel, even if no one else does. It is "the power of God"—more potent than any cosmic sign. And it is "the wisdom of God"—filled with enough eternal profundity to make all the wisdom of this world seem like mere foolishness by comparison.

But there is only one class of people who recognize the power and the wisdom of the gospel: "those who are the called"—the elect. They do respond to the gospel. Jesus said, "All that the Father gives Me *will* come to Me" (John 6:37, emphasis added). "My sheep hear My voice, and I know them, and they follow Me" (10:27). Those who are called effectually by the Holy Spirit do see and embrace both the wisdom and power of God in the gospel. That's why we must never overlay its simple message with political rhetoric, philosophical arguments, comedy routines, entertainment packages—or any other useless form of earthly wisdom.

What seems mere foolishness to the worldly mind is in reality the *only* instrument that can reach sinners and turn their hearts to Christ, because it is the wisdom and power of God. What's more, "the foolishness of God is wiser than men, and the weakness of God is stronger than men" (v. 25). In other words, heaven's "foolishness" isn't really foolish after all. No clever ploy, political strategy, or philosophical argument concocted by the cleverest human mind could ever add an iota of power to the unadorned truth of the gospel. Those who depart from the simplicity and purity of the gospel forfeit the only God-ordained means for reaching lost people and freeing them from the hopeless bondage of sin.

GOD'S GOOD PLEASURE

To add to or subtract from any aspect of gospel truth is to forfeit God's blessing. "God was well-pleased through the foolishness of the message preached to save those who believe." That is the pattern for ministry He ordained. Those who imagine they can improve on His plan gain only His displeasure.

It is crucial to understand that the disdain for human wisdom that resonates through these early chapters of 1 Corinthians is no mere personal preference of the apostle Paul's. He is being moved along by the Holy Spirit as he writes, and the truth of what he says comes directly from God. Preaching the gospel is not an experimental missionary strategy Paul is toying with. It is God's own master plan and sovereign purpose for evangelism and church growth. Paul describes it as a deliberate choice the Lord made with a distinct purpose in view. "God has chosen the foolish things of the world to shame the wise, and God has chosen the weak things of the world to shame the things which are strong, and the base things of the world and the despised God has chosen, the things that are not, so that He may nullify the things that are, so that no man may boast before God" (vv. 27–29).

Again, God is well-pleased with His strategy. Only the most shameless kind of sinful arrogance would lead someone to think the sovereign intention of God is deficient, or that His plan for redeeming sinners needs modification. But many today *have* brashly tried to modify it. Some throw all their energies and resources into schemes that aim to redeem society through politics. Others think the key to reaching people is some form of contextualization where the preacher morphs the gospel message into something the world will like: wise-sounding philosophical reasoning; nice-sounding moral platitudes; cool-sounding postmodern jargon; hip-sounding music; or whatever.

All of that is a distraction from the simple truth of the gospel, and to whatever degree the preacher buries the gospel message under pragmatic methodologies like those, he actually works against the power of the message he is called to proclaim. Even if such tactics draw bigger crowds, they can't possibly have the same powerful effect as the undiluted gospel preached plainly and straightforwardly. In practice, such tactics have multiplied false converts in the church, and that is one of the main reasons the evangelical movement today is in such a mess.

The church Paul wrote these words to was in a similar condition—polluted with worldly values, pagan ideas, and carnal sinfulness.

There is one solution to that, and it is the gospel—the message of the cross—specifically, the truth that Christ died for our sins and rose again for our justification. That is the truth we must believe, the hope we must cling to, and the message we must proclaim, not only to our unregenerate neighbors but also to each other—"not in cleverness of speech, so that the cross of Christ would not be made void" (1:17). And "not in persuasive words of wisdom, but in demonstration of the Spirit and of power, so that [our] faith would not rest on the wisdom of men, but on the power of God" (2:4–5). For the gospel itself is the power of God. It may seem like "foolishness to those who are perishing, but to us who are being saved it is the power of God" (1:18).